THE
NEW ENGLAND
INDIANS

C. KEITH WILBUR

The Globe Pequot Press

Old Saybrook, Connecticut

Library of Congress Catalogue Number: 78-61713
ISBN: 0-87106-004-3

Printed in the United States of America
First Edition, Tenth Printing

• Contents •

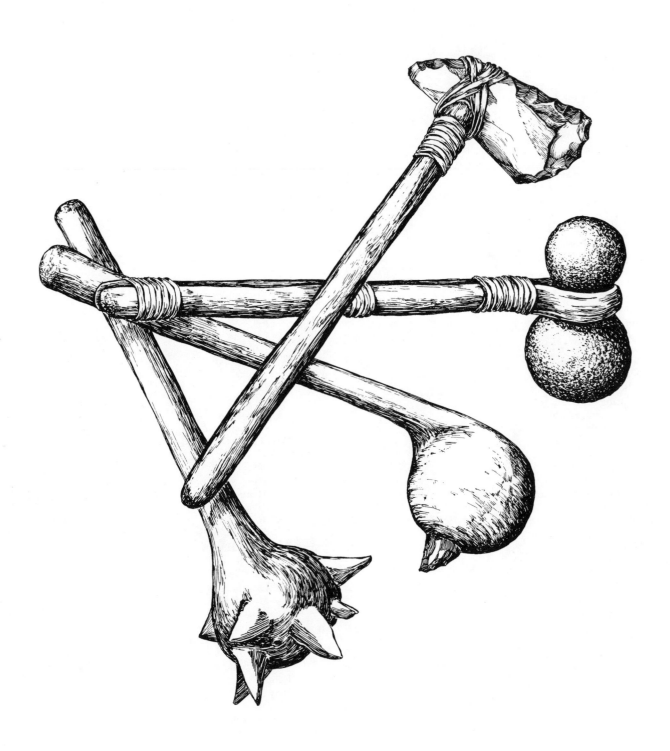

FOREWORD

The New England Indians have long been buried under a mass of indifference, prejudices, hearsay, Victorian ideas about "the noble red men," and guilt complexes over the racially downtrodden. Our television and movies have given the impression that the only American Indian was the western Indian, living against a backdrop of canyons, plains, galloping soldiers and whooping cowboys. If this sounds a bit extreme, witness the next Cub Scout pageant or the town's historical celebration. Full feathered war bonnets, spears, totem poles and a teepee village will be sure to add color ~ and a lack of authenticity ~ to the celebration. Our Algonquins would never recognize themselves!

Meanwhile, the archaeologists have been quietly working behind the scenes, trying to flesh out the prehistoric Indian and his way of life. Webster defines prehistory as "existing in times antedating written history." Without such records, the excavated arrowheads and other nonperishable implements must speak for themselves. Interpreting the find is all important, and one has little patience with the museum that designs an Indian head profile from a gathering of arrowheads and lets it go at that.

The earliest eyewitness accounts from sixteenth century traders and explorers introduced the Historic period. Their observations were recorded with pen and ink ~ fascinating accounts that would survive through later generations. The Pilgrims and the Puritans gave more specific writings of their wilderness neighbors ~ and with reasonably little distortion. When King Philip's War in 1675 ~ 1676 effectively dissolved these New Englanders and their more primitive cultures, their nine thousand years of living gradually faded from memory.

They deserve a better fate.

1

PALEO ~ INDIAN ~ 10,500± years ago.

13,500 years before today, New England slumbered under a blanket of ice, several miles in thickness. This gigantic deep freeze had begun to melt, gradually retreating to the St. Lawrence River area over the next thousand years. Meltwater released the sand and smoothly abraded rocks that had been absorbed by the glacial advance. High winds rearranged these deposits into an irregular, desolate landscape, fit for neither man nor beast.

EDGE OF ICE SHEET ~
① 13,500 YEARS AGO.
② 12,600 YEARS AGO.

Gradually, a summer of sorts took place ~ short, cold, wet and bleak. Trees from more southerly areas gained a root-hold to turn the sandy surface into a stubble of greenery. Primarily deciduous, spruce and fir trees multiplied, interspersed with scattered cedar, oak, birch and tamarack. But within a few hundred miles of the glacial base, only the tundra could survive. Stunted clumps of spruce and fir rose above a scattered growth of grasses, sedges and willows. Today, Cape Cod gives something of the feeling of those early times.

Game was the first to appreciate the fresh new look. There was lichen for the caribou in the tundra belt. Likely the mastodon and mammoth browsed there, and perhaps the musk ox, giant beaver, elk, deer and smaller rabbits as well.

New England's first people were strictly summer visitors. Earlier generations had migrated from Asia some 15,000 years ago. Moving in small bands by way of the iced-over Bering Strait route to Alaska, they followed game southward into the western United States. Nearly 5000 years later, their ancestors had made their way eastward to New England ~ and still on the hunt. They were nomads, leaving the area when the early snows came.

Although New England has yielded no skeletal remains of the Paleo people, it seems reasonable that they had Mongoloid characteristics. One might visualize them as having straight black hair, slanted eyelids, wide cheekbones, and shovel-shaped upper incisor teeth. Probably they wore skins from the hunt as protection from the heavy rains and snows.

These early hunters are assumed to be sailors of sorts. To reach those areas where the camps have been identified, they paddled across Long

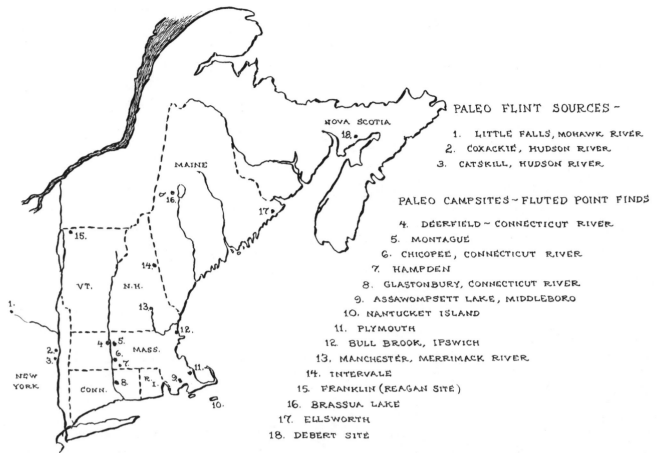

PALEO FLINT SOURCES ~

   1. LITTLE FALLS, MOHAWK RIVER
   2. COXACKIE, HUDSON RIVER
   3. CATSKILL, HUDSON RIVER

PALEO CAMPSITES ~ FLUTED POINT FINDS

   4. DEERFIELD ~ CONNECTICUT RIVER
   5. MONTAGUE
   6. CHICOPEE, CONNECTICUT RIVER
   7. HAMPDEN
   8. GLASTONBURY, CONNECTICUT RIVER
   9. ASSAWOMPSETT LAKE, MIDDLEBORO
   10. NANTUCKET ISLAND
   11. PLYMOUTH
   12. BULL BROOK, IPSWICH
   13. MANCHESTER, MERRIMACK RIVER
   14. INTERVALE
   15. FRANKLIN (REAGAN SITE)
   16. BRASSUA LAKE
   17. ELLSWORTH
   18. DEBERT SITE

Island Sound in dugouts to southern New England, probed inland along the Connecticut River and up along the Massachusetts coast. The discovered sites diminish to the northward along the Maine coast and on to Brunswick and Nova Scotia. Most of the campsites were along tributary streams and atop sandy plateaus.

    Likely the Paleo Indians roasted their meat over an open hearth ~ no stone fireplaces have been found. Springs, or a river hard by, supplied water for camp living. Temporary huts of brush and skin could be dismantled after the brief hunting season. The workshop was near the campsite, and it was there that many remarkable spear points were crafted.

FLUTED SPEAR POINTS ~

the Paleo hallmark. While admiring the finely chipped points, it is easy to forget that this sharp piece of flint meant survival to the ancient hunter. And flint they were ~ imported flint ~ for New England had no such outcroppings. Unearthed specimens are identical to quarried pieces from the Mohawk and Hudson River valley in New York State.

3

Many of these found points were brought by dugout as chunks of raw material, then chipped at the campsite workshop.

TECHNIQUE ~ A Paleo flintsmith might complete a fluted point in just half an hour! The average length averaged between $1\frac{3}{4}$ths to $3\frac{3}{4}$ths inches.

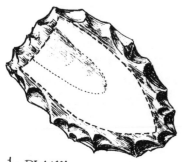

1. BLANK
×1

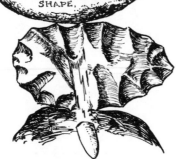

2. DIRECT PERCUSSION WITH HAMMERSTONE AGAINST EDGES. OUTSIZED EGG SHAPE.

3. SQUARING BASE. THE THINNER END WAS CHOSEN FOR THE BASE AND THE THICKER FOR THE POINT. THE BASE WAS GIVEN A SHARP BLOW AT RIGHT ANGLES TO THE BLANK.

CORRECT BASE.

4. IF BASE DID NOT SEPARATE AT 90°, IT MUST BE SQUARED.

5. ANGLED BASE (#4) WAS CHIPPED SQUARE OR GROUND FLAT.

6. FLUTING ~ BLANK WAS SET UPRIGHT ON ANVIL, BASE UP. ANTLER, BONE OR IVORY PUNCH WAS HELD FIRMLY NEAR BASE, STRUCK WITH HAMMER-STONE.

7. IF FLUTE NECK WAS NARROW AND BOTTLE SHAPED, SIDE FLAKES WOULD BE NECESSARY.

8. FLAKING WAS REPEATED ON THE OPPOSITE SIDE

9. IF BLANK WAS SUITABLE, IT WAS AGAIN FLAKED AND THE BASE SQUARED. IF FLUTES WERE NOT DEEP ENOUGH, THE PUNCH WAS USED AGAIN.

10. FINAL PRESSURE FLAKING WITH ANTLER, BONE OR IVORY TOOL.

11. BASE CURVED AND BASAL EDGES ABRADED SMOOTH. FINISHED!

PALEO HUNTING ~ Kill without being killed!

Probably no more than five families - about thirty individuals - made up each roving band. Occasionally, they would join with others for a hunting drive. Small, immature mastodons and mammoths might be speared after separation from the rest of the herd, or perhaps the herd was stampeded over a cliff or into the mire of a swamp. But no right-thinking hunter would try spearing one of these rampaging giants on equal terms. More likely, the fluted spear point found its mark in smaller game such as rabbits or birds.

MASTODON

MAMMOTH

THESE HUGE GRASS AND ROOT EATERS WERE EARLY RELATIVES OF THE ELEPHANT.

X 1

POSSIBLE SPEAR HAFTING.

OTHER PALEO TOOLS ~ a summary of other

Paleo site discoveries, including some speculation on how they were used. Drawn x ½ size.

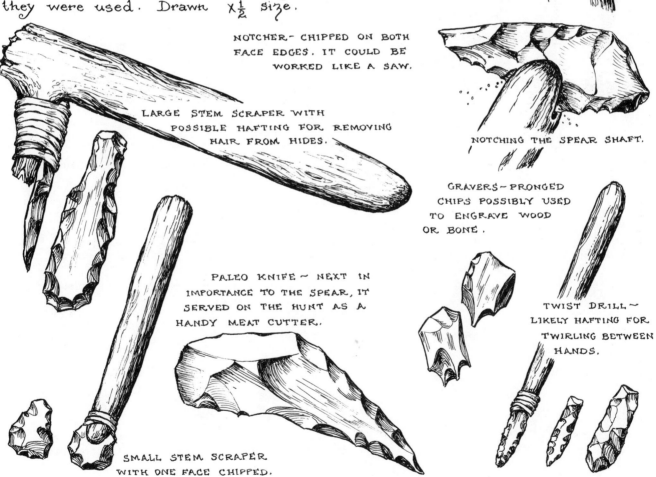

NOTCHER - CHIPPED ON BOTH FACE EDGES. IT COULD BE WORKED LIKE A SAW.

LARGE STEM SCRAPER WITH POSSIBLE HAFTING FOR REMOVING HAIR FROM HIDES.

NOTCHING THE SPEAR SHAFT.

GRAVERS ~ PRONGED CHIPS POSSIBLY USED TO ENGRAVE WOOD OR BONE.

PALEO KNIFE ~ NEXT IN IMPORTANCE TO THE SPEAR, IT SERVED ON THE HUNT AS A HANDY MEAT CUTTER.

TWIST DRILL ~ LIKELY HAFTING FOR TWIRLING BETWEEN HANDS.

SMALL STEM SCRAPER WITH ONE FACE CHIPPED.

5

EARLY ARCHAIC INDIANS ~ 7000~5000 years ago.

A changing New England~warm and dry~encouraged a better seeding for white and red pine, as well as such hardwoods as oak and beech. While the struggling jack pine, fir and spruce were gradually being replaced, there was enough lichen in the sur~ viving tundra to attract herds of caribou. Taking advantage of this antlered bonanza was a new breed of Indian~the Early Archaics.

EARLY ARCHAIC HEARTH~AN OPEN CIRCLE.

These new arrivals were of the same Asian background as the Paleo Indians, and likely their dress and dwellings were similar. But as hunters, they brought new and different methods of bringing down game. As they mingled with the older culture, the fluted point was modified and then replaced by the Early Archaic influx.

PROJECTILE POINTS ~ the most plentiful of Indian arti-
facts~are the surest identification of any culture period. Since necessity is the mother of invention, every projectile point was designed to meet the needs of its time. The evolution of the Early Archaic weapons is a case in "point."

As the Early Archaic influence gradually prevailed over the Paleo people, the old and honored fluted point underwent changes.

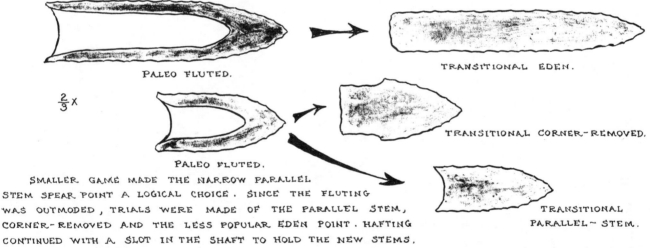

PALEO FLUTED.

TRANSITIONAL EDEN.

$\frac{2}{3}$ X

PALEO FLUTED.

TRANSITIONAL CORNER~REMOVED.

TRANSITIONAL PARALLEL~STEM.

SMALLER GAME MADE THE NARROW PARALLEL STEM SPEAR POINT A LOGICAL CHOICE. SINCE THE FLUTING WAS OUTMODED, TRIALS WERE MADE OF THE PARALLEL STEM, CORNER~REMOVED AND THE LESS POPULAR EDEN POINT. HAFTING CONTINUED WITH A SLOT IN THE SHAFT TO HOLD THE NEW STEMS.

THE EARLY ARCHAICS INTRODUCED A SPEAR POINT WITH A DEFINITE STEM. THE DEVELOPMENT OF THESE CORNER~REMOVED POINTS IS:

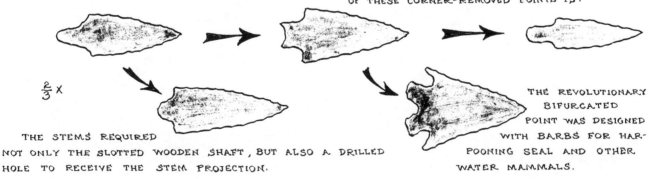

$\frac{2}{3}$ X

THE STEMS REQUIRED NOT ONLY THE SLOTTED WOODEN SHAFT, BUT ALSO A DRILLED HOLE TO RECEIVE THE STEM PROJECTION.

THE REVOLUTIONARY BIFURCATED POINT WAS DESIGNED WITH BARBS FOR HAR-POONING SEAL AND OTHER WATER MAMMALS.

6

HAFTING THE SPEARPOINT ~

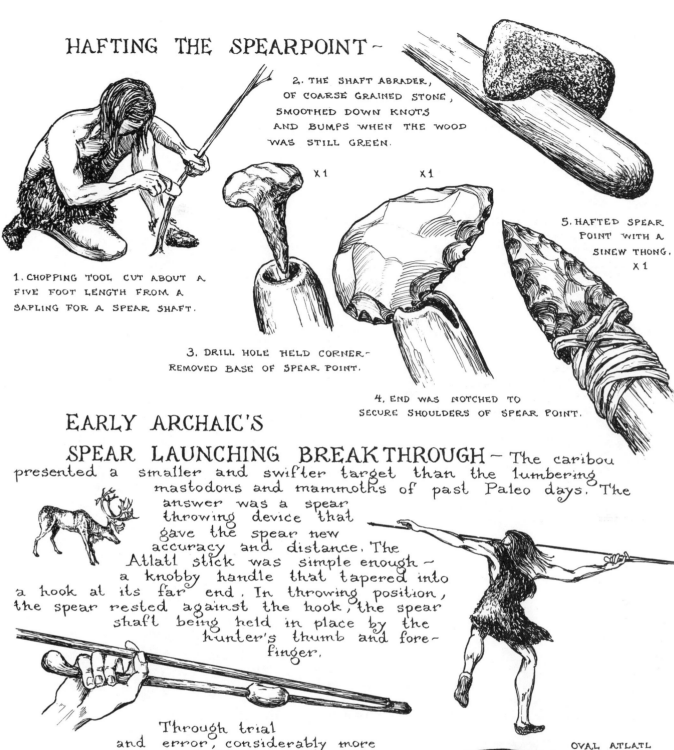

1. CHOPPING TOOL CUT ABOUT A FIVE FOOT LENGTH FROM A SAPLING FOR A SPEAR SHAFT.

2. THE SHAFT ABRADER, OF COARSE GRAINED STONE, SMOOTHED DOWN KNOTS AND BUMPS WHEN THE WOOD WAS STILL GREEN.

X 1

X 1

3. DRILL HOLE HELD CORNER-REMOVED BASE OF SPEAR POINT.

4. END WAS NOTCHED TO SECURE SHOULDERS OF SPEAR POINT.

5. HAFTED SPEAR POINT WITH A SINEW THONG. X 1

EARLY ARCHAIC'S

SPEAR LAUNCHING BREAKTHROUGH ~ The caribou

presented a smaller and swifter target than the lumbering mastodons and mammoths of past Paleo days. The answer was a spear throwing device that gave the spear new accuracy and distance. The Atlatl stick was simple enough ~ a knobby handle that tapered into a hook at its far end. In throwing position, the spear rested against the hook, the spear shaft being held in place by the hunter's thumb and forefinger.

Through trial and error, considerably more power was delivered by weighting the Atlatl stick. The Atlatl weight ~ formerly called a "bannerstone" ~ was a smooth oval stone with a slightly tapered hole drilled through its length. One outer face was grooved or flattened to allow the fingers to grasp the spear shaft. By pushing the weight over the hook ~ larger hole first ~ it became wedged on the tapered throwing stick.

OVAL ATLATL WEIGHT.

$\frac{5}{8}$"

$\frac{1}{2}$"

X 1

7

EARLY ARCHAIC HARPOON~

The bifurcated (notched base) point had its own built-in barbs, and was probably only for harpooning.

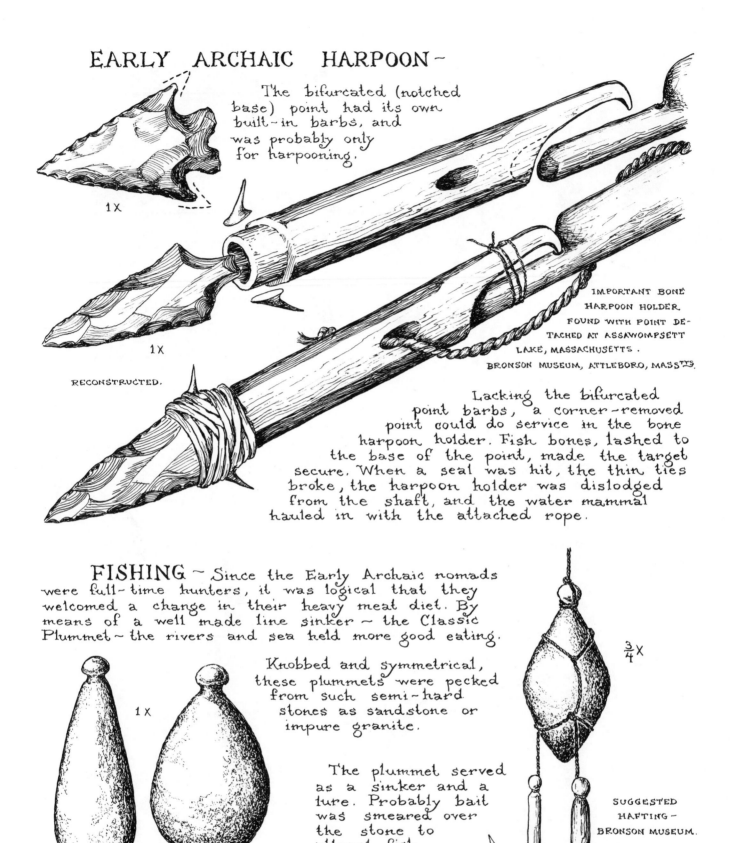

1 X

1 X

RECONSTRUCTED.

IMPORTANT BONE HARPOON HOLDER FOUND WITH POINT DE-TACHED AT ASSAWOMPSETT LAKE, MASSACHUSETTS. BRONSON MUSEUM, ATTLEBORO, MASSTS.

Lacking the bifurcated point barbs, a corner-removed point could do service in the bone harpoon holder. Fish bones, lashed to the base of the point, made the target secure. When a seal was hit, the thin ties broke, the harpoon holder was dislodged from the shaft, and the water mammal hauled in with the attached rope.

FISHING ~

Since the Early Archaic nomads were full-time hunters, it was logical that they welcomed a change in their heavy meat diet. By means of a well made line sinker ~ the Classic Plummet ~ the rivers and sea held more good eating.

Knobbed and symmetrical, these plummets were pecked from such semi-hard stones as sandstone or impure granite.

The plummet served as a sinker and a lure. Probably bait was smeared over the stone to attract fish.

1 X

CLASSIC PLUMMETS.

$\frac{3}{4}$ X

SUGGESTED HAFTING ~ BRONSON MUSEUM.

8

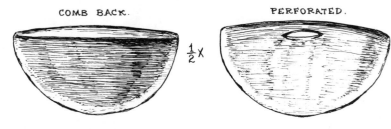

HUNTING ALLY ~
The wolf dog was the only domesticated animal of the Early Archaics.

ADVANCES IN CUTTING TOOLS ~

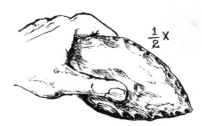

COMB BACK.

½ X

PERFORATED.

Leaf knife ~ this hunter's blade needed no handle.

The Ulu knife was for women's work ~ cutting meat, splitting fish for drying and cooking, skinning and dressing hides for bags, clothing and belts. The making and hafting of the Ulu is of interest:

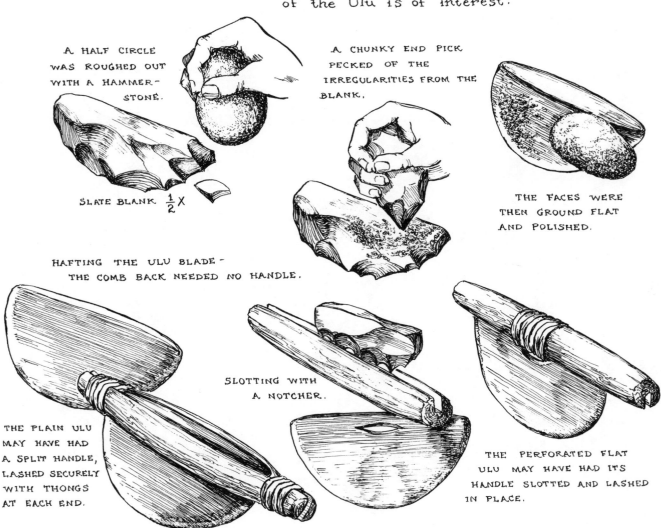

A HALF CIRCLE WAS ROUGHED OUT WITH A HAMMER-STONE.

SLATE BLANK ½ X

A CHUNKY END PICK PECKED OF THE IRREGULARITIES FROM THE BLANK.

THE FACES WERE THEN GROUND FLAT AND POLISHED.

HAFTING THE ULU BLADE ~ THE COMB BACK NEEDED NO HANDLE.

SLOTTING WITH A NOTCHER.

THE PLAIN ULU MAY HAVE HAD A SPLIT HANDLE, LASHED SECURELY WITH THONGS AT EACH END.

THE PERFORATED FLAT ULU MAY HAVE HAD ITS HANDLE SLOTTED AND LASHED IN PLACE.

9

OTHER TOOLS of the huntsman's trade.
CURING THE SKIN~

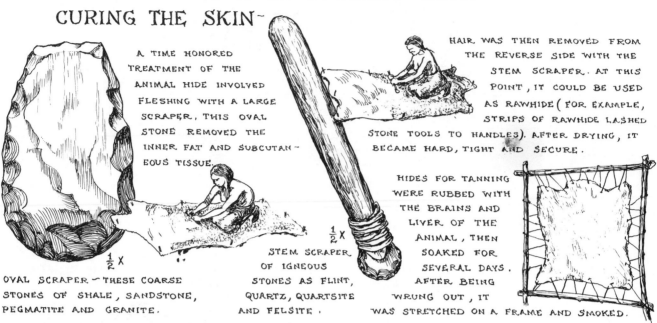

A TIME HONORED TREATMENT OF THE ANIMAL HIDE INVOLVED FLESHING WITH A LARGE SCRAPER, THIS OVAL STONE REMOVED THE INNER FAT AND SUBCUTANEOUS TISSUE.

½ X

OVAL SCRAPER~THESE COARSE STONES OF SHALE, SANDSTONE, PEGMATITE AND GRANITE.

½ X

STEM SCRAPER OF IGNEOUS STONES AS FLINT, QUARTZ, QUARTSITE AND FELSITE.

HAIR WAS THEN REMOVED FROM THE REVERSE SIDE WITH THE STEM SCRAPER. AT THIS POINT, IT COULD BE USED AS RAWHIDE (FOR EXAMPLE, STRIPS OF RAWHIDE LASHED STONE TOOLS TO HANDLES). AFTER DRYING, IT BECAME HARD, TIGHT AND SECURE.

HIDES FOR TANNING WERE RUBBED WITH THE BRAINS AND LIVER OF THE ANIMAL, THEN SOAKED FOR SEVERAL DAYS. AFTER BEING WRUNG OUT, IT WAS STRETCHED ON A FRAME AND SMOKED.

WOODWORKING with the Channeled gouge~ and fire.

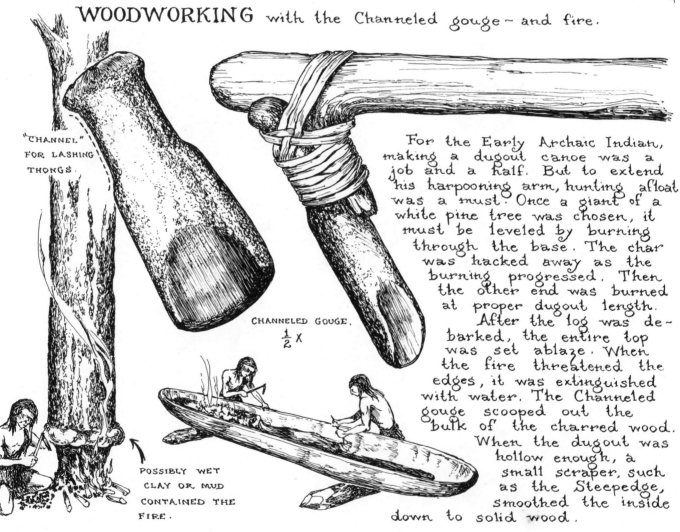

"CHANNEL" FOR LASHING THONGS.

CHANNELED GOUGE.
½ X

POSSIBLY WET CLAY OR MUD CONTAINED THE FIRE.

For the Early Archaic Indian, making a dugout canoe was a job and a half. But to extend his harpooning arm, hunting afloat was a must. Once a giant of a white pine tree was chosen, it must be leveled by burning through the base. The char was hacked away as the burning progressed. Then the other end was burned at proper dugout length.

After the log was debarked, the entire top was set ablaze. When the fire threatened the edges, it was extinguished with water. The Channeled gouge scooped out the bulk of the charred wood. When the dugout was hollow enough, a small scraper, such as the Steepedge, smoothed the inside down to solid wood.

LATE ARCHAIC INDIAN ~ 5000 years ago to 300 A.D.

Warm, dry weather had become the rule. The new forest spread rapidly over New England. Hardwoods were in the majority ~ elm, beech, hickory, chestnut and oak ~ with a scattering of spruce, pine and hemlock. Although there was little ground layer to cover the sandy ground, the fresh growth supported increasing numbers of white~tailed deer, moose, black bear, beaver, and turkey.

The caribou had moved northward into Canada, following the tundra and the melting glaciers. The Early Archaic hunters were right behind them, leaving their old camps to an entirely new culture. The Late Archaic Indians were just that, and their creative know-how was in marked contrast to the hand-to-mouth existence of their predecessors. They came in small bands from the Great Lakes area~ family oriented, peaceloving and a credit to the Indian peoples.

The Late Archaic Indians homesteaded New England in style. Their sizable circular buildings ranged from 30 to 66 feet in diameter. The cone~shaped roofs were likely sheathed with large bark shingles. An unusual entrance, enclosed by an extended wall, gave rise to the term "snail-shell" house.

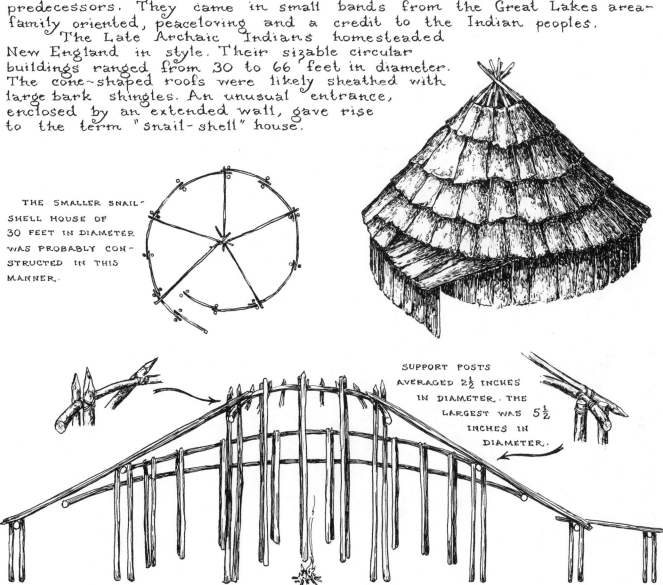

THE SMALLER SNAIL-SHELL HOUSE OF 30 FEET IN DIAMETER WAS PROBABLY CON-STRUCTED IN THIS MANNER.

SUPPORT POSTS AVERAGED 2½ INCHES IN DIAMETER. THE LARGEST WAS 5½ INCHES IN DIAMETER.

THIS LARGE CEREMONIAL LODGE AT ASSAWOMPSETT LAKE, MIDDLEBORO, MASSACHUSETTS WAS 66 FEET IN DIAMETER. A LARGE PIT WITHIN CONTAINED 11 SECONDARY BURIALS, FINE GRAVE GOODS AND RED OCHER. BRONSON MUSEUM DISPLAY.

11

WOMAN'S WORLD –

The squaw's lot improved considerably. In her comfortable lodgings, she took charge of the hearth and the preparation and cooking of the meal. Strike-a-light sets were her fire-making tools – either two lumps of iron pyrites or one lump of this mineral and one of flint. A shower of sparks into a tinder of "touchwood" or spunk (a growth from the black birch) started the blaze.

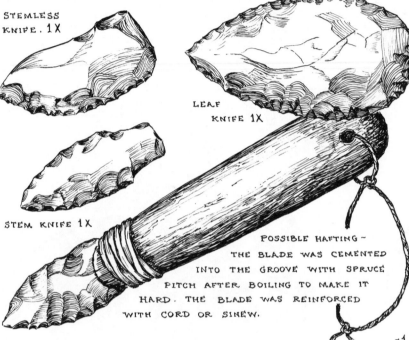

STEMLESS KNIFE. 1X

LEAF KNIFE 1X

STEM KNIFE 1X

POSSIBLE HAFTING – THE BLADE WAS CEMENTED INTO THE GROOVE WITH SPRUCE PITCH AFTER BOILING TO MAKE IT HARD. THE BLADE WAS REINFORCED WITH CORD OR SINEW.

PYRITE IS A CINDER-LIKE CRUST OF IRON CRYSTALS EMBEDDED IN SOME SUCH STONE AS QUARTZ.

The Late Archaic woman did not meet her household challenges overnight. At first, the knife was her only tool. It probably took all of a thousand years before she could offer her family anything but the old solid meat and fish diet with nuts and berries for variety. There were no containers for liquids – no cooking utensils – that could give a hearty stew to a hungry family.

STONE BOWL INDUSTRY –

It was a quiet beginning for the discovery of the century. Some tribesman must have experimented with an outcrop of steatite (soapstone) and found it could be easily worked with hard stone tools. The stone bowl industry was born, and life in New England was never again the same. Fine cooking kettles first made their appearance, and then followed a host of cooking and eating stoneware – drinking cups, spoons, platters, plates, dishes and storage bowls. Although most were of steatite, chlorite was also valued. Both stones owed their softness to the mineral talc that was part of their content.

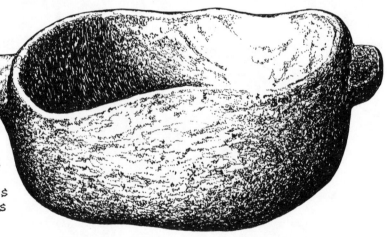

STEATITE COOKING KETTLE. $\frac{1}{2} - \frac{1}{3}$ X

12

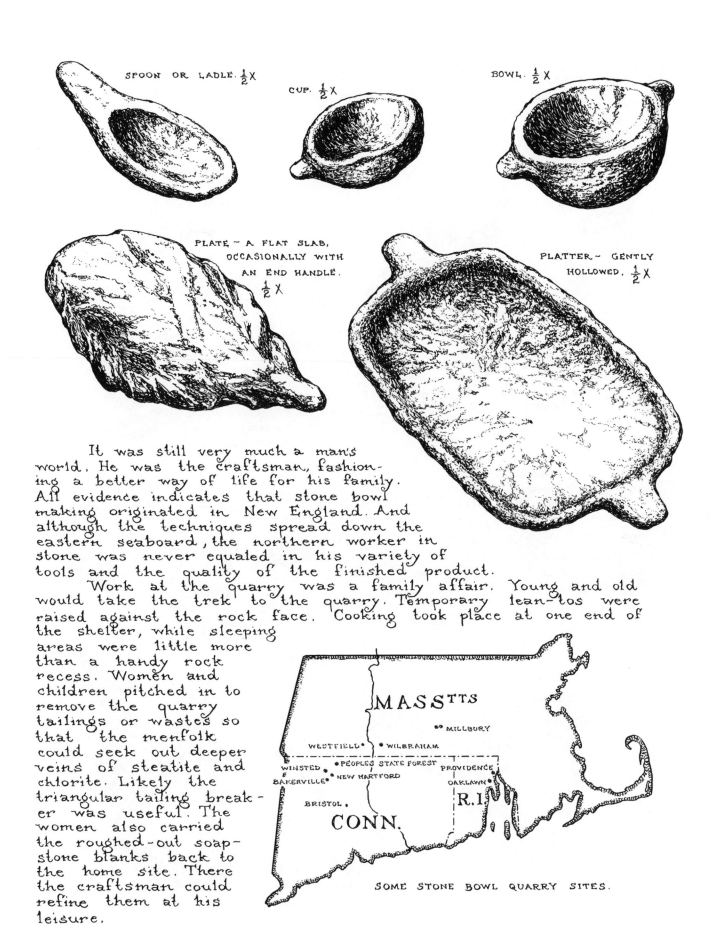

SPOON OR LADLE. ½X

CUP. ½X

BOWL. ½X

PLATE ~ A FLAT SLAB,
OCCASIONALLY WITH
AN END HANDLE.
½X

PLATTER ~ GENTLY
HOLLOWED. ½X

It was still very much a man's world. He was the craftsman, fashioning a better way of life for his family. All evidence indicates that stone bowl making originated in New England. And although the techniques spread down the eastern seaboard, the northern worker in stone was never equaled in his variety of tools and the quality of the finished product.

Work at the quarry was a family affair. Young and old would take the trek to the quarry. Temporary lean-tos were raised against the rock face. Cooking took place at one end of the shelter, while sleeping areas were little more than a handy rock recess. Women and children pitched in to remove the quarry tailings or wastes so that the menfolk could seek out deeper veins of steatite and chlorite. Likely the triangular tailing breaker was useful. The women also carried the roughed-out soapstone blanks back to the home site. There the craftsman could refine them at his leisure.

MASSTTS

MILLBURY

WESTFIELD • WILBRAHAM

WINSTED • PEOPLES STATE FOREST
• BAKERVILLE • NEW HARTFORD

PROVIDENCE

OAKLAWN

BRISTOL

R.I.

CONN.

SOME STONE BOWL QUARRY SITES.

13

BOWL-MAKING

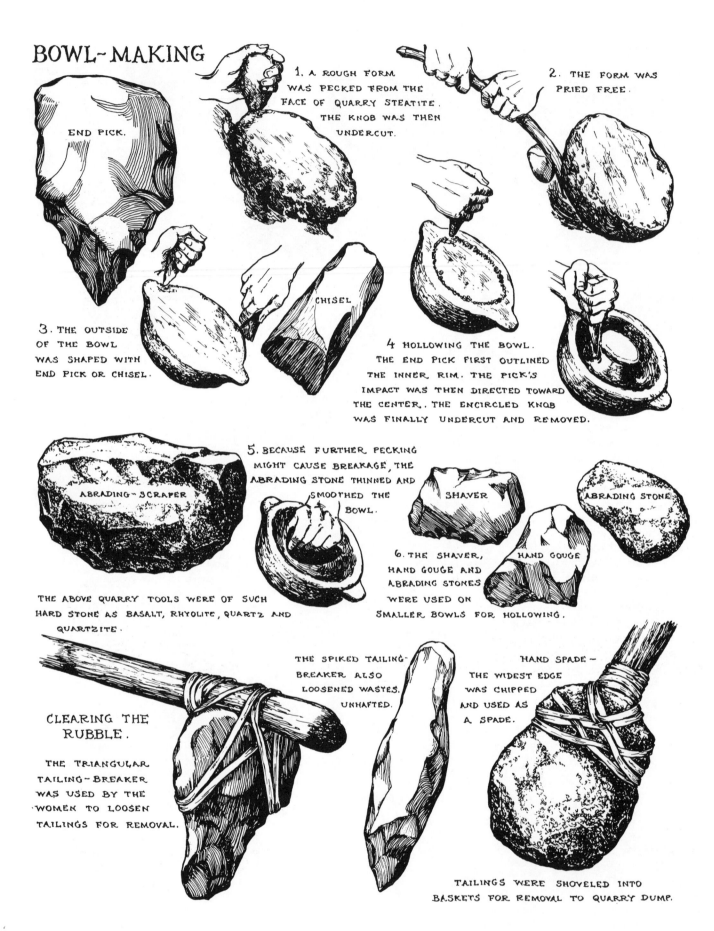

END PICK.

1. A ROUGH FORM WAS PECKED FROM THE FACE OF QUARRY STEATITE. THE KNOB WAS THEN UNDERCUT.

2. THE FORM WAS PRIED FREE.

3. THE OUTSIDE OF THE BOWL WAS SHAPED WITH END PICK OR CHISEL.

CHISEL

4 HOLLOWING THE BOWL. THE END PICK FIRST OUTLINED THE INNER RIM. THE PICK'S IMPACT WAS THEN DIRECTED TOWARD THE CENTER. THE ENCIRCLED KNOB WAS FINALLY UNDERCUT AND REMOVED.

5. BECAUSE FURTHER PECKING MIGHT CAUSE BREAKAGE, THE ABRADING STONE THINNED AND SMOOTHED THE BOWL.

ABRADING-SCRAPER

SHAVER

ABRADING STONE

HAND GOUGE

6. THE SHAVER, HAND GOUGE AND ABRADING STONES WERE USED ON SMALLER BOWLS FOR HOLLOWING.

THE ABOVE QUARRY TOOLS WERE OF SUCH HARD STONE AS BASALT, RHYOLITE, QUARTZ AND QUARTZITE.

THE SPIKED TAILING-BREAKER ALSO LOOSENED WASTES. UNHAFTED.

HAND SPADE — THE WIDEST EDGE WAS CHIPPED AND USED AS A SPADE.

CLEARING THE RUBBLE.

THE TRIANGULAR TAILING-BREAKER WAS USED BY THE WOMEN TO LOOSEN TAILINGS FOR REMOVAL.

TAILINGS WERE SHOVELED INTO BASKETS FOR REMOVAL TO QUARRY DUMP.

The soapstone quarries were a success ~ no doubt about it! With the liquid container problem solved, the inventive mind of the Late Archaic artisan turned to other necessities of that day. The soft stone could be handily worked into atlatl weights, plummets, effigies, pendants, gorgets, pipes and nut mortars.

NUT MORTARS ~

The new forest had produced a bounty of nuts. The squaw was quick to prize the meat of the walnut ~ and the oil that could be extracted. Acorns could be ground into meal for winter storage. Roots, seeds, berries and bone marrow could be pulverized into a mash and used to fortify the stews.

At first, a long, smooth cobblestone from the old glacial meltout gave reasonable service. This was succeeded by a pestle, never more than 10 inches in length, pecked from local sandstone, granite or schist. A mortar was a logical companion ~ at first little more than a pecked depression in a lump of steatite. Food preparation was becoming an art.

LATE ARCHAIC THICK-WALLED STEATITE MORTAR AND PESTLE. ½ X

NUT ANVILS HELPED REMOVE THE ARMOR-PLATED EDIBLES. ⅓ X

PIPES ~

The quarries were probably worked for a full 2000 years until displaced by clay pottery. About 100 years before this new medium was introduced (A.D. 200), a fresh influx of migrants from Ohio ~ the Adena people ~ brought new customs and traditions to New England. Pipe-smoking caught fire, and the soapstone craftsmen filled the new demand.

PLATFORM PIPE FORM. ½ X

STRAIGHT PIPE FORM. ½ X

ELBOW PIPE FORM. ½ X

1. THE PIPE BLANKS WERE FIRST ROUGHED OUT WITH A SMALL END PICK. THE THREE FORMS COULD MAKE USE OF PREVIOUSLY DISCARDED STEATITE CHUNKS.

3. THE MOST TICKLISH OPERATION ~ DRILLING THE STEM. A HARDWOOD STICK, ⅛ TH INCH IN DIAMETER, WAS LIKELY REVOLVED BETWEEN THE PALMS. DRILLING THIS NARROW HOLE WAS SLOW WORK. IT WAS SPEEDED BY ADDING FINE SAND FOR ABRASION.

¾ X

2. THE BOWL AND STEM WERE PECKED ROUND; THEN THE TOP OF THE BOWL AND END OF THE STEM WERE RUBBED FLAT WITH AN ABRADING STONE.

¾ X

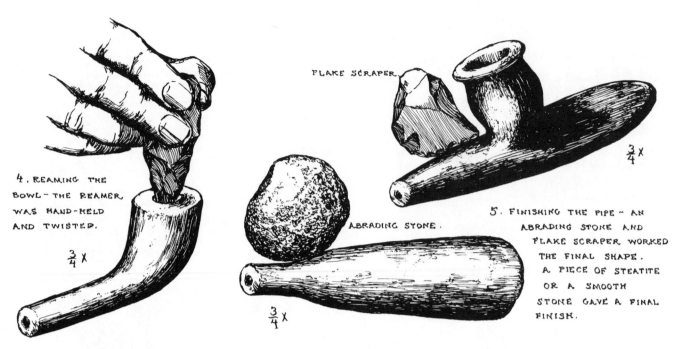

4. REAMING THE BOWL - THE REAMER WAS HAND-HELD AND TWISTED.

¾ X

FLAKE SCRAPER.

ABRADING STONE.

¾ X

5. FINISHING THE PIPE - AN ABRADING STONE AND FLAKE SCRAPER WORKED THE FINAL SHAPE. A PIECE OF STEATITE OR A SMOOTH STONE GAVE A FINAL FINISH.

Crafting the necessities and conveniences for Late Archaic living reached well beyond the steatite quarries. Special tools, chiefly of stone and rarely of copper and bone, were shaped according to use.

COPPER TOOLS

~ The Lake Superior region was well-known for its yields of pure copper nuggets. With their Great Lakes background, it was not surprising that an occasional workman owned a tool of this metal.

Cold copper could not be pounded extensively before small cracks would appear. By heating (annealing) the copper, then letting it cool, the metal could be shaped without injury. The heating and cooling process was repeated until the tool was completed.

WORKING THE COPPER.

The Indian had no knowledge of working iron. Therefore, any iron object had to be obtained from white traders. No iron in possession of a tribesman can date before the sixteenth century. Cast and sheet copper were also of European origin.

COPPER GOUGE, VERMONT

½ X

COPPER AX, MASSACHUSETTS.

½ X

COPPER PIN. CONNECTICUT

½ X

No copper ornaments have been found from this period.

16

BONE IMPLEMENTS

~ Toward the latter part of the Late Archaic period, bone tools were in demand. Bone awls were common and useful for making holes in skins before sewing with sinew or plant fibers. Awl holes were helpful in quill and basketwork, and used for peg holes in wood, shredding sinew, and engraving pictures in soft stone. It came in a nearly usable form, for the fibula of the deer needed only a bit of sharpening to make the tool.

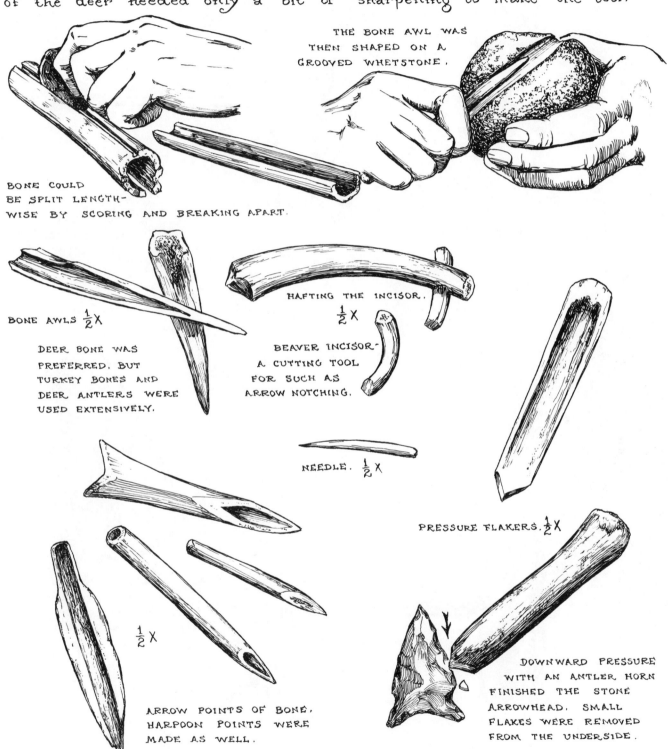

THE BONE AWL WAS THEN SHAPED ON A GROOVED WHETSTONE.

BONE COULD BE SPLIT LENGTHWISE BY SCORING AND BREAKING APART.

BONE AWLS ½ X

DEER BONE WAS PREFERRED, BUT TURKEY BONES AND DEER ANTLERS WERE USED EXTENSIVELY.

HAFTING THE INCISOR. ½ X

BEAVER INCISOR - A CUTTING TOOL FOR SUCH AS ARROW NOTCHING.

NEEDLE. ½ X

PRESSURE FLAKERS. ½ X

½ X

ARROW POINTS OF BONE, HARPOON POINTS WERE MADE AS WELL.

DOWNWARD PRESSURE WITH AN ANTLER HORN FINISHED THE STONE ARROWHEAD. SMALL FLAKES WERE REMOVED FROM THE UNDERSIDE.

17

WOODWORKING TOOLS -

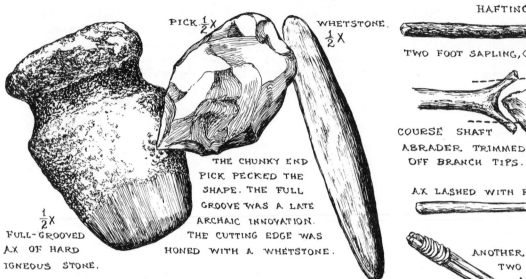

PICK. ½X   WHETSTONE. ½X

HAFTING.

TWO FOOT SAPLING, OPPOSITE BRANCHES.

NOTCHER CUT THE FORK TO FIT AX GROOVE.

COURSE SHAFT ABRADER TRIMMED OFF BRANCH TIPS.

THE CHUNKY END PICK PECKED THE SHAPE. THE FULL GROOVE WAS A LATE ARCHAIC INNOVATION. THE CUTTING EDGE WAS HONED WITH A WHETSTONE.

½X
FULL-GROOVED AX OF HARD IGNEOUS STONE.

AX LASHED WITH RAWHIDE.

ANOTHER HAFTING ~ TWO SAPLINGS, THINNED AT THEIR CENTERS FOR THE AX GROOVE WERE SOAKED BEFORE BINDING.

These larger full-grooved axes felled large trees with the aid of fire. Smaller axes leveled trees up to 6 inches in diameter for house poles, bed planks and platforms.

CUT, SOFTENED IN WATER, OR RAWHIDE WAS CRISSCROSSED FROM BLADE TO HANDLE.

AS WITH ALL HANDLES, THE BARK OF THE SAPLING WAS FIRST REMOVED. KNOTS WERE LEVELED WITH A ROUGHING KNIFE AND SMOOTHED WITH A SHAFT ABRADER. BUT WITH THE HATCHET, THE HANDLE NEAR THE BLADE WAS THINNED TO GIVE BETTER BALANCE.

HATCHET ½X ~ CHIPPED TO SHAPE, THEN THE CUTTING EDGE WAS GROUND.

CELT ½X
ANOTHER WOODCUTTER THAT WAS USED AS A CHISEL. SOME WERE HAFTED, OTHERS WERE STRUCK WITH A STONE.

THE HOLLOWING OF THE BLADE AND THE 1 OR 2 GROOVES ON THE BACK WERE FORMED WITH THE END PICK.

HAFTING THE GROOVED GOUGE.

GROOVED GOUGE ½X

18

Utilitarian~fine craftsmanship~ efficient~these were the hallmarks of the Late Archaic stone tools. With these, the woodworker was actually crafting bowls, platters, cups and dishes well before the steatite quarries were opened. Steepedge scrapers, notchers, shavers and small engraving blades indicate some of the effort put into turning out wooden vessels. The acid New England soil has not treated old wood kindly. A wealth of information about these early cultures has perished with the perishables.

PRESERVED WOODEN BOWL, ABOUT 4,300 YEARS OLD. BRONSON MUSEUM.

By careful detective work, an occasional wooden vessel has been salvaged. One well-known find was discovered on the southwest shore of Quaboag Lake, Brookfield, Massachusetts. The organic rot of a wooden bowl was preserved with a plastic spray. How a block of wood, removed from a sizable tree with only fire and a stone ax, could be transformed into this useful vessel remains a mystery.

OTHER TOOLS ~ The drill.

 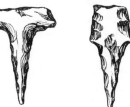   

HAFTING.

PLAIN.   T-BASE.   TAPERED-STEM.   EARED.   CROSS.   DIAMOND.   PIPE BOWL REAMER.

Find a full-grooved ax or a grooved gouge and you've found a Late Archaic site. The same applies to the drill point, for any of its many varieties would be specific for the period. A multi-media tool, it could bed the arrow in the shaft, drill the soapstone pipe, repair a stone bowl or perforate a gorget or a pendant.

Small diameter holes of greater depth needed a different twist. Back at the steatite quarry, a twirled hardwood stick was often in action. Hollow cane, a bone from a large wading bird, or a pithy stick of elderwood made reasonable drills. A small amount of wet sand was caught in the end of the drill to act as the abrasive. Rotated between the palms, a core was left in the center of the hole that could easily be broken off.

HUNTING ~ Those soapstone pots needed filling, and the ingenuity of the Late Archaic Indian was not found wanting. At first, the spear and its weighted throwing stick served the purpose when on the hunt. The old oval weight, however, had given way to carefully made weights in fanciful shapes. Colorful graining was highlighted by polishing. These highly valued pieces not only had stream-lined side wings to plane the air efficiently, but also served as a good luck charm for the hunter.

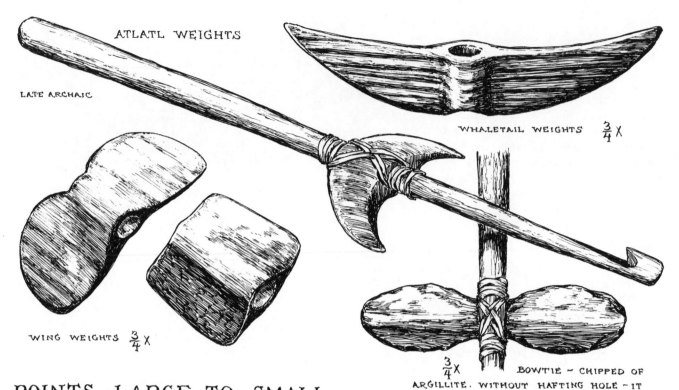

ATLATL WEIGHTS

LATE ARCHAIC

WHALETAIL WEIGHTS $\frac{3}{4}$ X

WING WEIGHTS $\frac{3}{4}$ X

$\frac{3}{4}$ X   BOWTIE ~ CHIPPED OF
ARGILLITE. WITHOUT HAFTING HOLE ~ IT
WAS LASHED TO THE ATLATL STICK.

POINTS ~ LARGE TO SMALL ~

Eared, side-notched, corner-removed, tapered stem~ these were
the spear points that characterized the Late Archaic period. But gradually a new and different point evolved ~ a smaller version of the
large spear heads that the past cultures had known. The bow and
arrow were here to stay as the backbone of the hunter's equipment.
Only the white man's musket would one day improve the accuracy and
distance of a nicely crafted arrow and a keen eye behind it.

The importance of the bow and arrow to Indian life deserves
far more than this brief introduction. But no early examples of these
wooden weapons remain ~ only the points and their hafting tools.
More on this when solid examples of the later Ceramic-Woodland
culture appear. Meanwhile, the progression of spear points to arrow
points would look something like this:

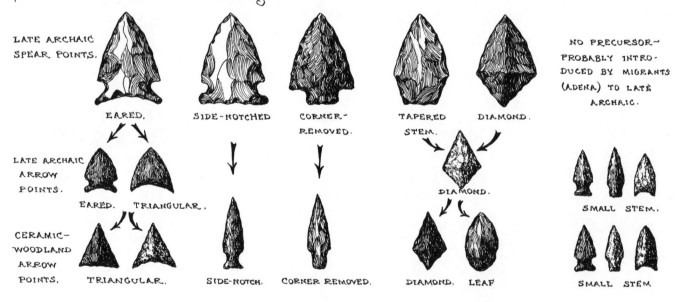

LATE ARCHAIC
SPEAR POINTS.

EARED.   SIDE-NOTCHED   CORNER-
REMOVED.   TAPERED
STEM.   DIAMOND.

NO PRECURSOR~
PROBABLY INTRO-
DUCED BY MIGRANTS
(ADENA) TO LATE
ARCHAIC.

LATE ARCHAIC
ARROW
POINTS.

EARED.   TRIANGULAR.   DIAMOND.   SMALL STEM.

CERAMIC-
WOODLAND
ARROW
POINTS.

TRIANGULAR.   SIDE-NOTCH.   CORNER REMOVED.   DIAMOND.   LEAF   SMALL STEM

"Points" of interest~

    The bow and arrow were imported from Asia. It seems reasonable that migrants from the west ~ the Adena people from Ohio, 500 B.C. or earlier ~ introduced this all-important means of hunting to the Late Archaics. They also likely hafted many of the arrows with the Small Stem arrow point.

    The New Englanders knew a good thing when they saw it. Spear hunting had seen its day, but one of their earliest spearpoint designs, the eared blade was reduced to fit the smaller diameter of the arrow shaft. The Tapered Stem and Diamond shapes became a smaller diamond. The later Ceramic-Woodland cultures saw fit to continue with the Triangular, Diamond and Small Stem points, and in addition skinned down the old Side-Notched and Corner-Removed types.

LATE ARCHAIC KNIVES $\frac{5}{8}$ X

STEMLESS AND
ASYMMETRICAL KNIFE.

STEM KNIVES,
SYMMETRICAL
AND LARGE STEMS.

    Spear or arrow point? In general (and generalizations are risky!), the larger the point and the wider the stem, the more likely that it saw duty as a spear. But if the point be in the Ceramic-Woodland form, it would be arrow or knife, not spear. They were rare indeed.

    Knife blades are tricky, unless they are asymmetrical with a single cutting edge. Then its a knife. As for symmetrical blades, they can mimic small or large arrow points. If a stem is present, it should be large enough to accommodate a handle. Check for wear on the edges of the blade as evidence of possible use as a cutting tool.

FISHING ~ Catching fish continued in the Early Archaic

way ~ with the bait-smeared plummet weight. But in contrast to the earlier nicely pecked weights, the Late Archaic stone-smith pounded out a crude copy to answer the purpose. Sometimes it was little more than a knobbed pebble. It was certainly a "Clumsy Plummet" that showed little pride in workmanship ~ perhaps because enthusiasm was lacking for an earlier invention.

    Other make-do plummets included a grooved and a perforated glacial cobblestone. First glance would give the impression of fish net weights, but there is no evidence that this culture had developed netting for this purpose.

CLUMSY
PLUMMET.
$\frac{1}{2}$ X

GROOVED
WEIGHT.
$\frac{1}{2}$ X

PERFOR-
ATED
WEIGHT
$\frac{1}{2}$ X

21

Therefore they are believed to be quick substitutes for the plummet and used as such.

Fish weirs — a remarkable discovery was made during the excavation for the New England Life Insurance building in Boston. Fish weir stakes, about 4000 years old, were evidence of Late Archaic fishing methods. High tide brought in the fish that then became trapped in the weir.

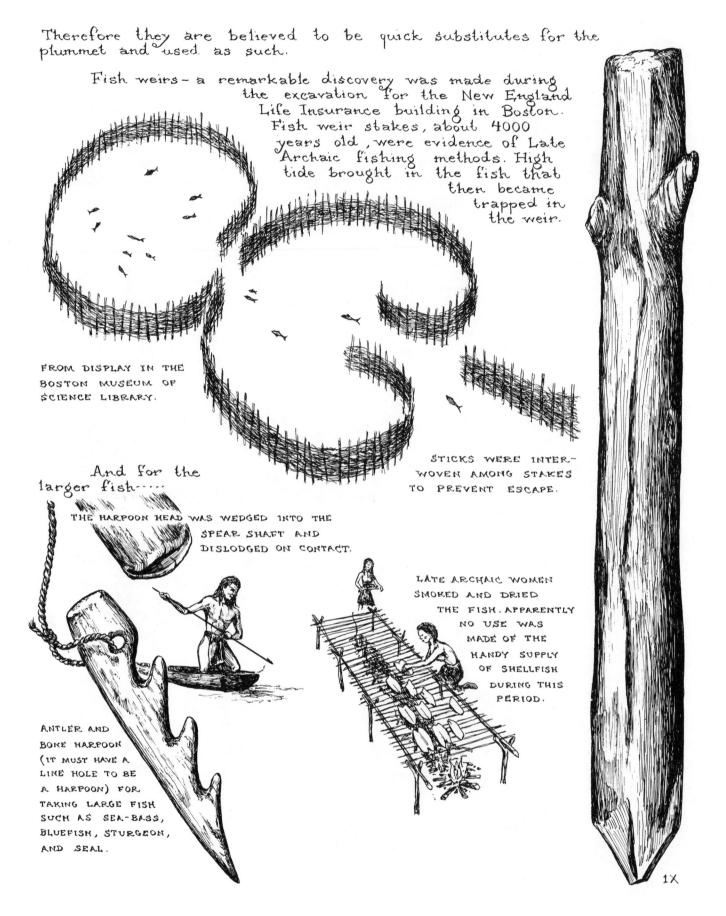

FROM DISPLAY IN THE BOSTON MUSEUM OF SCIENCE LIBRARY.

STICKS WERE INTER-WOVEN AMONG STAKES TO PREVENT ESCAPE.

And for the larger fish.....

THE HARPOON HEAD WAS WEDGED INTO THE SPEAR SHAFT AND DISLODGED ON CONTACT.

LATE ARCHAIC WOMEN SMOKED AND DRIED THE FISH. APPARENTLY NO USE WAS MADE OF THE HANDY SUPPLY OF SHELLFISH DURING THIS PERIOD.

ANTLER AND BONE HARPOON (IT MUST HAVE A LINE HOLE TO BE A HARPOON) FOR TAKING LARGE FISH SUCH AS SEA-BASS, BLUEFISH, STURGEON, AND SEAL.

1X

22

THE SPIRIT WORLD

~ It seemed reasonable enough to the Late Archaic Indian that his windfalls and downfalls were controlled by the spirits. What else but a displeased spirit could throw down lightning bolts, growl with thunder and howl in the winds? And when pleased, supply a bounty of game or fish to the hungry? There was no want of these unseen forces. They were everywhere ~ in the smallest stone or animal to the largest mountain or tree.

To have the best of two worlds ~ the here and the hereafter ~ a prudent Indian must respect the spirit world. He must show honor and pay homage to the kindly spirits or surely fall victim to the merciless powers of the evil ones. Disgrace, illness or death could be his lot. He needed someone in tune with the spirits to intercede for him ~ to bring him into the good graces of the good spirits and to drive out the evil powers that tortured him.

The shaman, or medicine man, assumed this duty with enthusiasm. If his rituals and techniques were strange to the bedeviled, they were pleasing to the powers he addressed. Only through this middleman could all be made right again. Religion hasn't changed all that much!

Death ~ that final journey into the unknown ~ required extraordinary preparations by the shaman. The Late Archaic deceased likely awaited his life after death during a drying period in a ceremonial lodge.

PENDANT ~
DUXBURY, MASS.
BRONSON MUSEUM.

THE THUNDERBIRD CREATED THUNDER BY THE FLAPPING OF ITS WINGS. LIGHTNING STRUCK EARTHWARD WITH THE OPENING AND CLOSING OF THE EYES. RAIN CAME FROM A LAKE IN ITS BACK.

HUMAN EFFIGIES. $\frac{3}{4}$ X

BELCHERTOWN, MASS^{TTS}
AMHERST COLLEGE MUSEUM.

EFFIGIES ~ LATE ARCHAIC?

RHODE ISLAND ~
ROGER WILLIAMS
PARK MUSEUM.

PECKED PEBBLE.
NARRAGANSETT BAY DRAINAGE
BRONSON MUSEUM.

WELLFLEET,
MASS^{TTS}
PEABODY MUSEUM,
CAMBRIDGE.

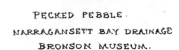
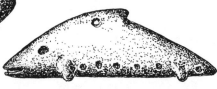

FISH EFFIGY, SCITUATE, MASS^{TTS}.
BRONSON MUSEUM, ATTLEBORO, MASS^{TTS}.

FISH EFFIGY, NARRAGANSETT BAY.
BRONSON MUSEUM.

Meanwhile, the shaman had prepared the sacred cremation site, usually on a sandy elevation well above and away from the living quarters. The ceremony, as reconstructed by archeological research, began with a fire in the cremation pit. The dried bones, wrapped in animal skins, were cast into the flames. Functional tools — gouges, arrowheads, axes, knives and such, were added to the blaze in sacred union with the dead. Magic stones, but rarely ornaments, followed the tools that could mean survival in the spirit world.

GRINDING SLABS OF SANDSTONE RANGED FROM 6" X 12' TO 8" X 12". PRIOR HEATING OF HEMATITE CHUNKS MADE FOR EASIER GRINDING AND A MORE BRILLIANT RED.

$\frac{3}{4}$ X

MAGIC STONES — IT IS BELIEVED THESE HANDSOME STONES — CRYSTALS, AND MULTICOLORED STONES — HELPED DRIVE THE EVIL SPIRITS AWAY.

After the cremation fire had cooled, the shaman transferred the charred remains to a nearby secondary burial pit. Red ochre powder was added to give blood and renewed energy in the later life. Discovery of a red ochre burial with cremation remains and period tools is proof positive of a Late Archaic burial site.

GORGETS ~
Occasionally, a sturdy ovoid stone with two central holes found its way into the cremation pit. This was not surprising, for there is no doubt that the gorget was a highly valued part of the Late Archaic's world. But there is doubt about its use. Possibilities include a badge of office, an important ceremonial trapping, or simply an ornament. Another interesting but less likely possibility — an arm guard with the bow and arrow.

IF THE GORGET WERE USED AS A WRIST GUARD, THE CROSSWISE STRAPPING WOULD SURELY TANGLE WITH THE BOW-STRING. THE POSITION OF THE TWO HOLES PREVENT A MORE USABLE LENGTHWISE POSITION.

LATE ARCHAIC GORGET 1 X

THE ADENA CULTURE~

Far to the west, the Adena Indians along the Ohio Valley were having their problems. A heavy influx of the Hopewell people from Illinois threatened their customs and convictions of their ancestors. This was intolerable to many of the more independent tribesmen~ enough so to leave their homelands for parts east. By 500 B.C. small numbers had infiltrated into New England ~ and quietly absorbed into the Late Archaic way of life.

Some of their belongings, drawn below, scarcely caused a ripple among their Late Archaic neighbors. They were certainly prized by their owners ~ and were to be found in Adena ~ connected cremations for the journey to the spirit world. Their pipe smoking caught on as previously mentioned, and pipes were produced in some quantity in the last days of the soapstone quarries.

But the greatest gift to the soapstone bowl makers was destined to make the Late Archaic handiwork obsolete and to forge a whole new culture ~ the Ceramic~Woodland. The ability to turn a common lump of clay into a ceramic pot or other useful article would bring enrichment ~ and disaster~ to the New England Indian.

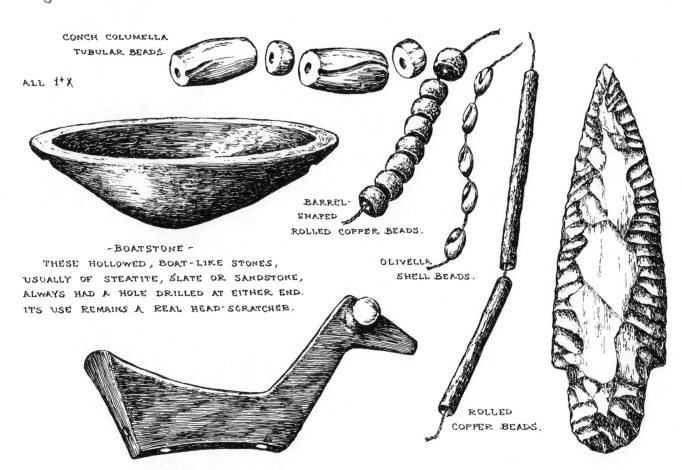

CONCH COLUMELLA
TUBULAR BEADS.

ALL 1+X

BARREL-
SHAPED
ROLLED COPPER BEADS.

OLIVELLA
SHELL BEADS.

~BOATSTONE~
THESE HOLLOWED, BOAT-LIKE STONES,
USUALLY OF STEATITE, SLATE OR SANDSTONE,
ALWAYS HAD A HOLE DRILLED AT EITHER END.
ITS USE REMAINS A REAL HEAD-SCRATCHER.

ROLLED
COPPER BEADS.

~BIRDSTONE~
THIS RARE SITTING BIRD OF SLATE OR SANDSTONE
USUALLY HAS PROMINENT, OFTEN PROTRUDING EYES AND
HOLES ANGLED AT EACH END OF THE BASE. ITS USE IS
AS MYSTERIOUS AS ITS DESIGN.

ADENA SPEAR POINT
WITH LARGE OVATE
EXTENDED STEM.

25

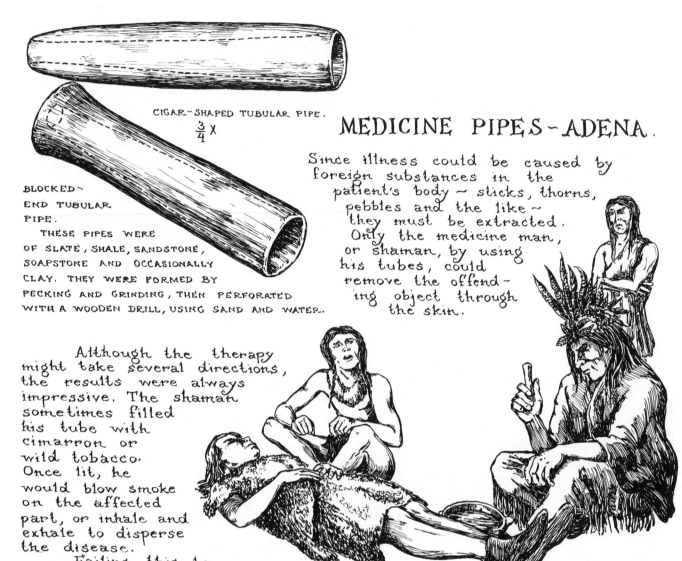

CIGAR-SHAPED TUBULAR PIPE.
$\frac{3}{4}$ X

BLOCKED-
END TUBULAR
PIPE.
THESE PIPES WERE
OF SLATE, SHALE, SANDSTONE,
SOAPSTONE AND OCCASIONALLY
CLAY. THEY WERE FORMED BY
PECKING AND GRINDING, THEN PERFORATED
WITH A WOODEN DRILL, USING SAND AND WATER.

MEDICINE PIPES ~ ADENA.

Since illness could be caused by foreign substances in the patient's body ~ sticks, thorns, pebbles and the like ~ they must be extracted. Only the medicine man, or shaman, by using his tubes, could remove the offend- ing object through the skin.

Although the therapy might take several directions, the results were always impressive. The shaman sometimes filled his tube with cimarron or wild tobacco. Once lit, he would blow smoke on the affected part, or inhale and exhale to disperse the disease.

Failing this, he might seat himself by the patient and begin his medicine song, keeping time with a rattle. Be- fore him was a bowl containing water and three tubes. One was removed and used to suck out the illness. The skin might first be abraded with a sharp flint for easier passage. Suddenly, and to the obvious distress of the doctor, he seemed to swollow the tube. When his agonies had ended, a lengthy speech followed. The shaman returned to his song and rattle, punctuating the whole with blows to his head, chest, sides and back. During this frenzy of activity, he occasionally strained as if to vomit the tube.

If the disease object still resisted these efforts, another tube was selected. It was also sucked upon and apparently swallowed. As the climax approached, one of the tubes was disgorged. More singing and rattling followed, and then ~ the second of the tubes appeared. Inside was the offending object ~ perhaps a feather. This was displayed to all. The shaman had again triumphed over disease.

THE QUIET REVOLUTION ~

For over five thousand years, the Late Archaic people had their share of peace and plenty. It was a good life. At least the women folk had some small degree of status as homemakers. In their sturdy homes they brewed soups of meat and fish. Their pots were fashioned with pride and patience by the men at the soapstone quarries. The stone bowl industry had been an advance of no mean proportion.

At first, the Adena settlers from the west seemed to have little impact on New England. Their mysterious birdstones and boat-stones were shrugged off by their Late Archaic neighbors. But their ability to fashion pots and utensils from common clay soon made the soapstone bowl obsolete. And they had a revolutionary new vegetable for those new pots ~ maize that was grown from their imported seeds. By 300 A.D., a whole new culture revolved about ceramics and agriculture. The tribesmen of this Ceramic-Woodland period were known as Algonquins.*

Bright prospects indeed ~ but with an unusual twist. The squaw became the backbone of this change in life styles, quietly assuming the skills necessary to produce clayware. She also carried on the back-breaking chores of farming, from planting until the last ear of corn was harvested. Sizable villages grew about the cleared fields. When this bounty brought raids from envious neighbors, stockades were erected for defense. The Indian way of life had become less quiet and more complicated.

The former stone craftsmen ~ the men of the tribe ~ had become warriors. Through the years, they pursued a bloody course of destruction. Long before the first white settlers came to New England's shores, intertribal wars were tearing apart the very fabric of Algonquin life.

* ALGONQUIAN (OR ALGONKIAN) TRIBES SHOULD NOT BE CONFUSED WITH THE SMALL ALGONKIN GROUP OF WESTERN QUEBEC IN CANADA.

27

CERAMIC ~ WOODLAND INDIANS ~ 300 A.D. to 1676 A.D.

New England has never wanted for changeable weather. The early Algonquins found it so, for cool and moist air had settled over the countryside. Conifers and hardwoods grew rapidly into big timber. A heavy accumulation of humus followed. It was this enriched soil that supported the farming efforts of the squaw.

GROWING THE CROP ~
Corn~ the basic edible of the Ceramic-Woodland culture ~had its modest beginnings as a wild grass. Archeologists have traced its origins from south central Mexico. By crossing strains, the early Indian farmers produced a small hybrid. These three inch or larger ears were introduced to New England by the Adena people from Ohio. At some time between 300 A.D. and 1500 A.D., the corn had tripled in size. Fertilization had made this change in good eating possible. Stalks of six to eight feet tall were bearing ears eight to nine inches in length, according to Governor Winthrop of the Massachusetts Bay Colony. He also made note of the kernel colorings of "...yellow, white, red, blue, olive, greenish, black, speckled, striped, etc.."

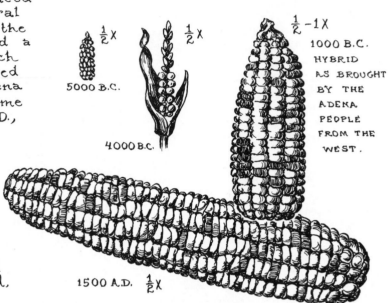

$\frac{1}{2}$ X
5000 B.C.

$\frac{1}{2}$ X
4000 B.C.

$\frac{1}{2}$ ~1X
1000 B.C. HYBRID AS BROUGHT BY THE ADENA PEOPLE FROM THE WEST.

1500 A.D. $\frac{1}{2}$ X

Clearing the land was man's work. Trees up to six inches in diameter could be felled without fire. Otherwise the heavier timber must be leveled with a base fire. The charcoal was easier to ax out than solid wood. If time were no object, the bark could be girdled and left to decay.

Grooveless axes were characteristic of the Algonquin period. Larger axes were cutting tools. Smaller sizes were both implements and weapons. Grooved axes were in use, but were less popular in the Ceramic-Woodland period.

BRONSON MUSEUM.

BLADE. 7$\frac{3}{4}$"

THE POPULAR CELT WAS WEDGE-SHAPED AND FITTED SNUGGLY INTO ITS HAFT. THIS FINE EXAMPLE WAS FOUND EIGHT MILES FROM NEW BEDFORD, WELL PRESERVED UNDER SALT WATER AND SAND. HAFT= 27$\frac{1}{2}$".

Several other grooveless wood-choppers were used during this period.

The smaller hafted specimen, the hatchet, has a ground cutting edge. Likely it was first used by the Late Archaics, then favored by the Ceramic-Woodland Algonquins. Light and efficient, it felled small trees for stockades, planks for beds, wigwam frames, and platforms. As intertribal wars built up momentum, it did execution as that dreaded sidearm, the tomahawk.

HATCHET. $\frac{3}{8}$ X

$\frac{3}{8}$ X

CHIPPED AX.

The husky chipped ax was hafted in the same way. Its appearance and function would appeal to today's woodsmen.

Ground breaking~

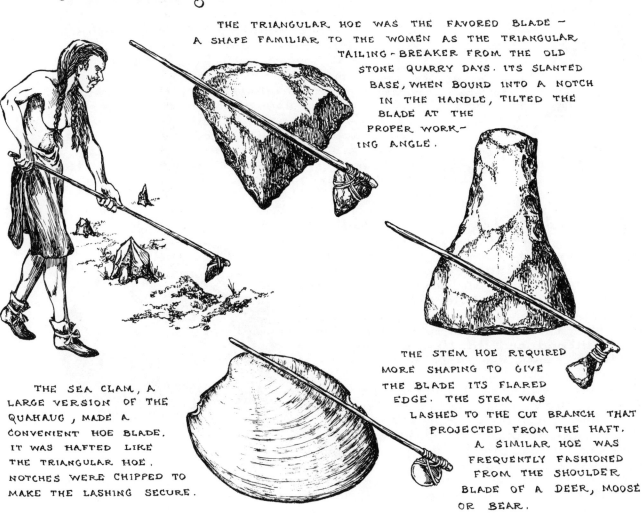

THE TRIANGULAR HOE WAS THE FAVORED BLADE — A SHAPE FAMILIAR TO THE WOMEN AS THE TRIANGULAR TAILING-BREAKER FROM THE OLD STONE QUARRY DAYS. ITS SLANTED BASE, WHEN BOUND INTO A NOTCH IN THE HANDLE, TILTED THE BLADE AT THE PROPER WORKING ANGLE.

THE STEM HOE REQUIRED MORE SHAPING TO GIVE THE BLADE ITS FLARED EDGE. THE STEM WAS LASHED TO THE CUT BRANCH THAT PROJECTED FROM THE HAFT. A SIMILAR HOE WAS FREQUENTLY FASHIONED FROM THE SHOULDER BLADE OF A DEER, MOOSE OR BEAR.

THE SEA CLAM, A LARGE VERSION OF THE QUAHAUG, MADE A CONVENIENT HOE BLADE. IT WAS HAFTED LIKE THE TRIANGULAR HOE. NOTCHES WERE CHIPPED TO MAKE THE LASHING SECURE.

29

Gardening was woman's work. Most of the early European writing place the squaw on the business end of the hoe. It comes as something of a surprise that Roger Williams saw the turning of the sod as a community project. "With friendly joyning they breake up their fields. They have a very loving sociable speedy way to dispatch it. All the neighbors, men and women forty, fifty, a hundred etc. joyne and come in to help freely." But once the soil had been prepared and divided into family plots, the woman was on her own.

POINTED.

FLAT.

THE STEM SPADE HAD ITS BEGINNINGS IN THE STEATITE QUARRIES AS THE HAND SPADE. BY NARROWING THE STEM, THE BLADE COULD BE LASHED TO A HANDLE.

ALTHOUGH AT FIRST GLANCE IT RESEMBLES A HOE, THE STEM SPADE HAS A THINNER AND FLATTER SURFACE. THE EDGE MIGHT BE ONE OF THESE THREE VARIETIES.

OVAL STEM HOE.

The planting season began when the leaves of the white oak were as large as a mouse's ears. Oval hills of dirt were piled up in a straight line – about three feet apart. By alternating the placement of each hill in succeeding rows, a like distance was maintained. It took a practiced eye to keep the planting pattern when old tree stumps littered the field.

Bigger and better crops called for fertilizer. Fish were plentiful enough during the spring spawning runs – two or three herring or a like fish were buried in each hill. Horseshoe crabs, as inedible as they are homely, made a tolerable fertilizer when chopped into bits. By enriching the soil, the three inch corn nubbin that was first introduced to New England grew to three times its original size.

Governor Winthrop recorded the multi-colored corn ears that delighted his fellow colonists. The English were quick to learn the Indian planting technique. Four kernels were placed in each hill (perhaps in recognition of the four directions of travel. Present day New Englanders continue this tradition.) Corn planting continued until the middle of June. In this way the squaw could harvest the April planting in

30

August, May plantings in September, and June's in October. For an early treat, the green corn stalk was sucked like sugar cane for its sweet juice.

The corn stalk served an additional function. When three or four kidney beans (Phaseolus vulgaris) were planted in the same hill, the stalk became a climbing pole for the bean vines. When mature, the colors were typically Indian — white, black, red, yellow, blue and spotted.

Squash and pumpkins were part of the colorful produce. Also planted in the hill, their vines grew out to sun between the mounds.

A small but hardy variety of tobacco (Nicotiana rustica) was planted and tended by the men. Common gardening was felt beneath their station. Their tobacco fields extended as far north as the Kennebec Valley.

HAND PLANTER. $\frac{1}{3}$X

VARIED SHAPES.

CORN-PLANTER. $\frac{1}{3}$X

At harvest time, the husks were stripped from the ripe corn and spread on mats to dry. If the corn was not ripe when gathered, it was boiled on the ear, shelled and dried on mats or bark strips. It would keep indefinitely.

Grain barns were dug into the slope of sandy hills, five or six feet deep. Corn on the cob was packed into large woven grass baskets, or in hollow logs cut into sections. Mats were banked around the sides and the tops of the containers, then the whole covered with three or four feet of sand. This cache of good eating was ready for the lean winter months. There was also the variety of other foods that had been squirreled away — dried beans, acorns, nuts, dried berries, dried meat, fish and shellfish.

THE CARRYING BASKET HUNG AT THE SQUAW'S BACK, SUPPORTED BY A STRAP THAT PASSED ACROSS THE CHEST. AS CORN EARS WERE PICKED, THEY WERE TOSSED OVER THE SHOULDER AND INTO THE BASKET. WHEN FILLED, IT WAS EMPTIED INTO A LARGER BASKET ON THE EDGE OF THE FIELD AND BROUGHT TO THE WIGWAM.

YET ANOTHER PLANTER — A LONG POINTED STICK. SOMETIMES A BRANCH WAS LEFT AS A FOOTREST.

It was just such a grain barn that helped sustain the Pilgrims during their 1620 exploration of Cape Cod. One of the caches held "…a fine great new Basket full of very faire corne of this yeare, with some 36 goodly ears of corne, some yellow and some red, and others mixt with blew which was a very goodly sight; the Basket was round, and narrow at the top, it held about three or four Bushels, which was as much as two of us could lift up from the ground, and was very handsomely and cunningly made."

MORTARS AND PESTLES ~ ALL DRAWN $\frac{1}{8}$ X

THE FIRST MORTARS WERE STURDY PRODUCTS FROM THE SOAPSTONE QUARRIES. SOMETIMES A GEODE WOULD SERVE THE PURPOSE. THESE HEAT-HARDENED SHELLS ENCLOSED A CRYSTALLINE CENTER THAT COULD BE KNOCKED FREE. BUT LOG MORTARS WERE PREFERRED AND IN GENERAL USE.

STEATITE MORTAR.

GEODE.

SHALLOW STONE.

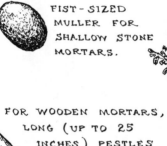

READY-FOR-USE GLACIAL COBBLE PESTLES USED WITH THE STONE MORTARS.

FIST-SIZED MULLER FOR SHALLOW STONE MORTARS.

LOG MORTAR.

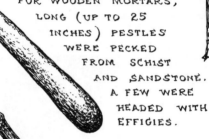

FOR WOODEN MORTARS, LONG (UP TO 25 INCHES) PESTLES WERE PECKED FROM SCHIST AND SANDSTONE. A FEW WERE HEADED WITH EFFIGIES.

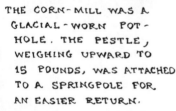

THE CORN-MILL WAS A GLACIAL-WORN POT-HOLE. THE PESTLE, WEIGHING UPWARD TO 15 POUNDS, WAS ATTACHED TO A SPRINGPOLE FOR AN EASIER RETURN.

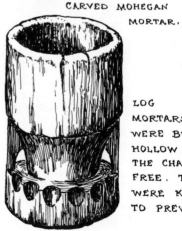

CARVED MOHEGAN MORTAR.

LOG MORTARS WERE BURNED HOLLOW AND THE CHAR SCRAPED FREE. THE SIDES WERE KEPT WET TO PREVENT BURNING.

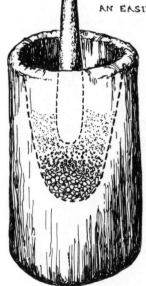

BECAUSE THE CAVITY WAS FUNNEL-SHAPED, UNCRUSHED KERNELS GRAVITATED TO THE CENTER TO RECEIVE THE FULL FORCE OF THE PESTLE. SMALLER PARTICLES ROSE TO THE TOP OF THE MORTAR.

FOOD PREPARATION~

CORN~ Green corn, a favorite, was prepared by roasting or boiling.

CORN MUSH OR SAMP~ Dry corn was broken into course grains, then boiled with currents into a paste. It was served plain or fried in fat. A favorite with the early colonists.

CORN MEAL CAKES~ Corn meal dough, sometimes mixed with dried berries, was molded into cakes. Each was wrapped in a leaf and baked in the hot ashes.

JOURNEY CAKE ~ could be prepared quickly and carried by the Indians on a long journey. Pounded corn meal was moistened and placed on a shaved clapboard from three to four inches wide and from fifteen to twenty inches long. This was best made on a red oak "jonny-cake" board. The putty-like glob was baked by the hearth until both sides were well done.

In the town of Warren, Rhode Island, Pokanoket's grist mill still stands. The mill was a natural flat table rock into which grooves were either cut or worn with use. Women of the Wampanoag tribe ground their corn by rolling round stones over the grain. (The millstone was rolled like a wheel with a shaft thrust through a hole in the center.) In this way they made the original Rhode Island Johnny Cakes.

"NO-CAKE"~ was made from pounded parched Indian corn. (The kernels were parched over hot ashes, then ground.) A warrior could carry forty days provisions of "no-cake" without inconvenience. It could be eaten with a little water, hot or cold. Every brave carried a small basket of this Nokehick at his back or in a hollow leather belt about his middle — enough for three or four days.

HOMINY ~ was whole or cracked corn with hulls removed by steeping in lye made from wood ashes. After rinsing and boiling in clear water, the kernels were ready for eating.

POPCORN~ An Indian treat, quickly appreciated by the colonists.

SUCCOTASH ~ made with corn and beans boiled with fat. Fresh or dried fish were sometimes added. Succotash was flavored and thickened with powdered walnuts, chestnuts or acorns.

STEWS~ The stew pot was a catch-all for anything that was digestible. Fish and game were cut into pieces — bones, entrails and all. Cleanliness was quite secondary to quantity. Corn, corn meal, beans, pumpkin, squash and roots gave a measure of variety. Stew bones were crushed with stone hammers — the bones settled to the bottom of the clay pot when the meat boiled off. To thicken, husked, dried and powdered acorns, chestnuts, and walnuts were added.

BEANHOLE BEANS ~ Baked beans were here well before there was a Boston. A fire was built in a pit that was lined with stones. When the stones were well heated, the embers were replaced with a pot of beans, well soaked — with perhaps maple syrup for flavoring.

SQUASH ~ All of it was eaten, including the seeds and blossoms. These found their way into any simmering stew.

CLAMBAKE ~ Here was a favorite way to cook shellfish — with the taste of the sea in every mouthful. Rocks were heated by building a fire upon them. When the embers were scraped free, clams, fish and green corn were placed on the hot rocks. Then seaweed covered the whole to contain the heat until the feast was thoroughly baked.

GROUNDNUTS (Apios tuberosa).
Common in moist thickets, this climbing
perennial plant has fragrant
chocolate brown flowers followed
by bean-like pods. The tubers grow
on thread-like roots and
resemble potatoes — about the
size of a hen's egg. The Indians
roasted or boiled the ground-
nut, or mashed them into ground-
nut cake. It was baked before the
open fire on flat rocks. They helped the Pilgrims survive the
winter of 1623.

GROUND NUTS.

JERUSALEM ARTICHOKE (Original was Helianthus tuberosus L.)
This close cousin to the sunflower
has roots that can be peeled and
sliced for salads or cooked as a
vegetable. The Indians cultivated
the plant in their gardens.

JERUSALEM
ARTICHOKE.

BERRIES ~ Strawberries,
blackberries, blueberries and
whortleberries were plentiful.
Eaten fresh or dried.

HICKORY NUTS were
crushed, shells and all, and mixed with water. The
oil rose to the surface and was preserved.

ACORNS of the white oak were shelled and
ground. The bitter principle was removed by boiling with lye
made with rotten maplewood ashes. The clear, sweet oil that rose
to the surface was skimmed off and eaten with meat or used
for anointing.

WALNUT meat was crushed in a little water and a small
amount of fine corn meal added. This mixture was boiled and
used as a substitute for mother's milk.

MAPLE SYRUP ~ Sugar making began
about the middle of March and lasted
a month. The spile was frequently
of slippery elm, inserted at the
base of a large "Y" cut in the
sugar maple bark.

THE BARK LOLLIPOP WAS
FILLED WITH MAPLE SUGAR.
SOMETIMES IT WAS FILLED WITH
SNOW AND MAPLE SYRUP POURED
OVER IT — AN EARLY "ICE CREAM CONE"
FOR THE CHILDREN. ½ X
(MAY BE HISTORIC).

MAPLE SAP DISH OF
ELM BARK, SCRAPED
SMOOTH AND BOUND
WITH INNER
BARK STRIPS.
½ - ⅓ X

BIRCH BARK SAP DISH.

34

CONTAINERS ~

Harvest time created a need for food containers. These varied from the simple sap collectors to intricately woven sweet grass baskets. These squaw-crafted trays, cups, dishes, pails, kettles, baskets, boxes and bags were often as handsome as they were utilitarian. Although western examples of these fragile containers have dated back to 9000 years, time and our acidic New England soil have lost all but a few from the relatively recent colonial contact period.

BARK CONTAINERS ~

The best tree-sheathing came from white birch, elm, chestnut, basswood, ash, cedar, fir and spruce. It could be stripped in the spring when the sap was flowing. Two cuts encircled the trunk - sometimes up to nine feet apart. A third cut connected the others down the length of the trunk. The bark sheet was pried free at the third cut with a sturdy stick, beveled at one end like a chisel. No tree could survive even a small denuding of this sort, but there was no lack of raw material in the Algonquin forest.

White birch, although at its best in northern New England, was preferred throughout the area. Josselyn made note that "Delicate sweet dishes too they make of Birch-Bark sowed with threads drawn from Spruse or white Cedar-Roots, and garnished on the out-side with florisht works, and on the brims with glistering quills taken from the Porcupine, and dyed, some black, others red, the white are natural, these they make of all sizes from a dram cup to a dish containing a pottle, likewise Buckets to carry water or the like, large Boxes too of the same materials······Kettles of Birchen-bark."

Gookin wrote that "Their pails to fetch their water in, are made of birch barks, artificially doubled up, that hath four corners and a handle in the midst. Some of these will hold two or three gallons and they will make one of them in an hours time."

It is surprising that those bark kettles were sometimes used for boiling. A hot meal instead of a snuffed fire depended on hanging the bark kettle a proper distance from the flame.

FOLDING THE BARK WAS MADE EASIER BY FIRST PLACING IT IN HOT WATER.

SPLINT BASKETS ~

MAPLE.

WHITE OAK.

HICKORY.

BLACK ASH.

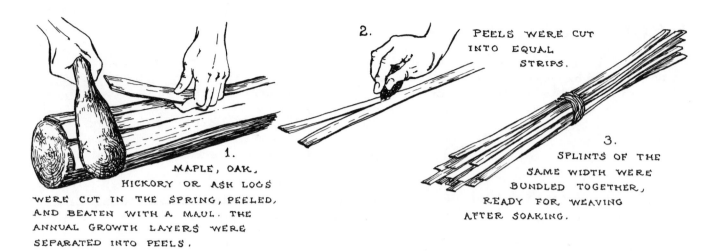

1. MAPLE, OAK, HICKORY OR ASH LOGS WERE CUT IN THE SPRING, PEELED, AND BEATEN WITH A MAUL. THE ANNUAL GROWTH LAYERS WERE SEPARATED INTO PEELS.

2. PEELS WERE CUT INTO EQUAL STRIPS.

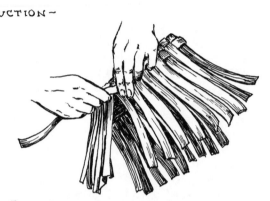

3. SPLINTS OF THE SAME WIDTH WERE BUNDLED TOGETHER, READY FOR WEAVING AFTER SOAKING.

~POSSIBLE CONSTRUCTION~

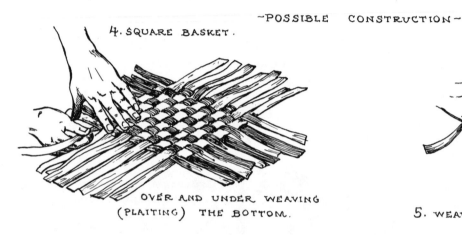

4. SQUARE BASKET.

OVER AND UNDER WEAVING (PLAITING) THE BOTTOM.

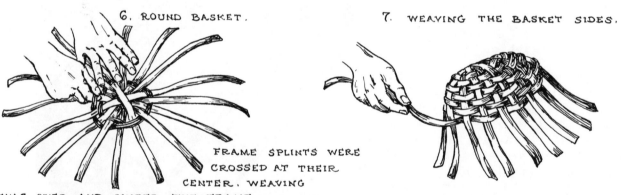

5. WEAVING THE SPLINT SIDES.

6. ROUND BASKET.

FRAME SPLINTS WERE CROSSED AT THEIR CENTER. WEAVING WAS OVER AND UNDER THE FRAME.

7. WEAVING THE BASKET SIDES.

BASKET SIEVES WERE NEARLY SQUARE ~ ABOUT ONE FOOT WIDE AND 4-5 INCHES DEEP WITH FLARING SIDES. THE BOTTOM WEAVE WAS WOVEN OF COARSE OR FINE SPLINTS, DEPENDING ON THE COARSENESS OF CORN MEAL DESIRED.

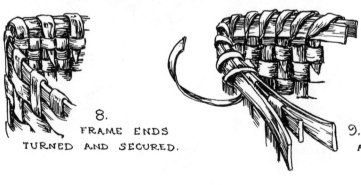

8. FRAME ENDS TURNED AND SECURED.

9. TWO SPLINTS ENCIRCLED THE RIM AND WERE LASHED TO STRENGTHEN IT.

36

COILED BASKETS ~

BONE AWL ~ $\frac{1}{2}$X

BONE AWLS FOR BASKET-MAKING WERE FORMED FROM SPLINTERED BONES. THE LEG BONE (ULNAR) OF THE DEER AND ALSO THE LEG BONES AND HUMERUS OF THE TURKEY WERE FAVORITES. THE BROAD END MAY HAVE BEEN WRAPPED IN SKIN.

THE AWL PUNCHED A HOLE IN THE PRECEEDING COIL. THE HEMP THREAD WAS PUSHED THROUGH AND OVER THE OUTSIDE COIL IN A CONTINUOUS SPIRAL.

Gookin wrote in 1674 that "Several sorts of baskets, great and small, some of them hold four bushels or more, and so on downward to a pint······ Some of these baskets are made of rushes and some of bents (coarse grass), others of maize husks, others of a kind of silk grass, others of a kind of wild hemp, and some of barks of trees. Many of these are very neat and artificial, with the portraiture of birds, beasts, fishes, and flowers upon them in colours."

Josselyn noted "Baskets, bags and mats, woven with bark of the lime tree and rushes of several kinds, dyed as before, some black, blue, red and yellow."

TWINED BASKETS ~

HEMP IN AND OUT WEAVING.

RUSHES WOVEN WITH HEMP.

ALGONQUIN PIPE BAG OF INDIAN HEMP, WITH ORNAMENTS OF FALSE EM-BROIDERY OF PORCUPINE QUILLS. COLORS ARE LIGHT NATURAL TO A DYED PURPLISH-BLACK.

IN AND OUT WEAVE.

Twined baskets were made of vertical warps, held together by several horizontal wefts that twined about each other. The twined wefts were woven in and out of the warps.

A favored twining material was Indian hemp. Prior to our present century, the hemp plant peppered the New England countryside. Now outlawed, we know it as marijuana.

HEMP TYING CORD FOR BAG HANDLE OR A RUNNING CORD FOR CLOSING THE MOUTH OF THE BAG.

(FROM WILLOUGHBY)

THREAD AND CORDAGE were made of Indian hemp, wild
flax, milkweed, as well as the inner bark of basswood swamp ash and others. Fibers of the latter were first shreaded from the bark before being twisted into thread or twine. The bark material was used for little more than narrow burden straps and an occasional bag.

SINGLE STRAND THREAD (ONE PLY).

THE "S" TWIST (LEFT TWIST).

FIBERS WERE ROLLED BACK AND FORTH UNDER THE PALM AGAINST THE THIGH. THIS TECHNIQUE DATES BACK TO THE ARCHAIC (AND POSSIBLY PALEO) DAYS. IT FOUND EARLY USE AS FISH LINES AND STRING FOR TYING. IT WASN'T VERY STRONG.

SPINDLE AND WHORL MAY HAVE BEEN USED IN NEW ENGLAND AS IT WAS IN THE SOUTHWEST. THE SPINDLE, WITH ITS PERFORATED WEIGHT, WAS SPUN AGAINST THE THIGH TO PRODUCE THREAD.

1X POSSIBLE WHORL.

DOUBLE STRAND (TWO PLY). TWO "S" TWISTED THREADS WERE TWISTED TOGETHER IN A "Z" TWIST OR RIGHT TWIST. IT THEN BECAME CORDAGE. CORDAGE WAS EXTENSIVELY USED FOR FISH NETS, BAGS, STRINGING BEADS, AND IN MAKING CORD-MARKED POTTERY.

COILED NETTING BAG OF CORD.
ABOUT 3X   (WILLOUGHBY)

EMBROIDERY ~ WOVEN CORD CONTAINERS OR CLOTHING COULD BE FANCIED UP WITH QUILLS OR ANIMAL HAIR. QUILLS RAN TO ABOUT 5 INCHES IN LENGTH. WHEN SOAKED IN WATER, EACH COULD BE TWISTED AND BENT QUITE HANDILY.

WRAPPING QUILL ON
CORD STITCHING.

PORCUPINE QUILLS WERE WRAPPED ONE AROUND EACH TWIST.

MOOSE HAIR WAS WRAPPED 3 TIMES AROUND EACH TWIST.

FOLDED QUILL ON
CORD STITCHING.

POTTERY INDUSTRY -

Women had firmly established their productivity and creativity as time moved through the Ceramic-Woodland period. She had taken up the business of growing crops and raising blisters, saw to the harvesting, then cooked or stored her efforts in her finely wrought containers. At the outset of the period, she was able to convert common clay into uncommon ceramic pots. The stone bowl industry, dominated by male craftsmen, had become obsolete. Here was New England's first Women's Liberation movement!

PREPARING THE CLAY -

WETTING AND KNEADING THE CLAY.

POWDERING THE CLAY.

SIFTING OUT THE LUMPS AND PEBBLES.

ADDING TEMPER OF CRUSHED STONES CONTAINING CONSIDERABLE QUARTZ AND FELDSPAR, CRUSHED BURNED SHELLS AND/OR PLANT FIBERS. THE TEMPER FROM CRACKING WHILE DRYING AND FIRING.

SHAPING THE POT -

A LUMP OF CLAY IS MOLDED TO FORM THE BASE OF THE POT.

THE BASE IS SECURED IN A SAND POCKET, PROTECTED BY STRIPS OF BARK.

MOIST CLAY ROLLED AND COILED ATOP THE BASE TO BUILD UP THE SIDES.

A WOODEN PADDLE, WOUND WITH CORD, BLENDS THE COILS OF CLAY TOGETHER.

EXTERIOR-

STAGES I, II, III, IV USED THE HEMP CORD TO WORK THE COILS INTO A SOLID SURFACE. STAGES III + IV USED THE HAND OR SMOOTHING TOOL TO SMOOTH OUTSIDE.

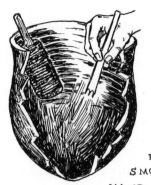

INTERIOR -

STAGE I USED THE CORD PADDLE WIPING. STAGES II, III, IV USED A PRONGED STICK TO BETTER JOIN THE COILS. THE ROUGHENED INSIDE WAS THEN SMOOTHED WITH THE HAND OR SMOOTHING TOOL.

DESIGN~

Algonquin pot decorations were simple enough. The earliest~ Stage I ~ had none. The cord-wiping had to do. Decorations developed as the craftswomen perfected their work. These were some of the design tools:

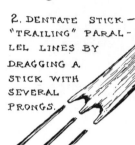

2. DENTATE STICK ~ "TRAILING" PARALLEL LINES BY DRAGGING A STICK WITH SEVERAL PRONGS.

STAGE II + III.

STAGE II.

"PUSH-PULL" WITH MULTI-PRONGED DENTATE STICK.

PLATTED ~ DENTATE WITH DENTATE STONE. STAGES II + III.

LINE ~ DENTATE. STAGES II, III, IV.

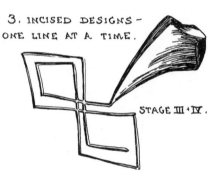

1. ROCKER ~ STAMP. THE EDGE OF THE SHELL WAS ROCKED BACK AND FORTH. STAGE II.

3. INCISED DESIGNS ~ ONE LINE AT A TIME.

STAGE III + IV.

FIRING ~

AFTER DRYING FOR SEVERAL DAYS, A FIRE WAS BUILT ON A BED OF FLAT STONES. WHEN REDUCED TO COALS, THE POT WAS LAID MOUTH TO THE HEAT UNTIL IT BROWNED LIGHTLY.

THE POT WAS ROLLED ONTO THE EMBERS AND COVERED WITH DRIED BARK. AFTER AN HOUR THE BARK HAD BURNED AND THE POT FIRED,

THE HOT POT WAS REMOVED AND DRIED PITH THROWN INSIDE. THE BURNING, SMOKING PITH BLACKENED AND WATERPROOFED THE INSIDE.

POT COMPARISON~

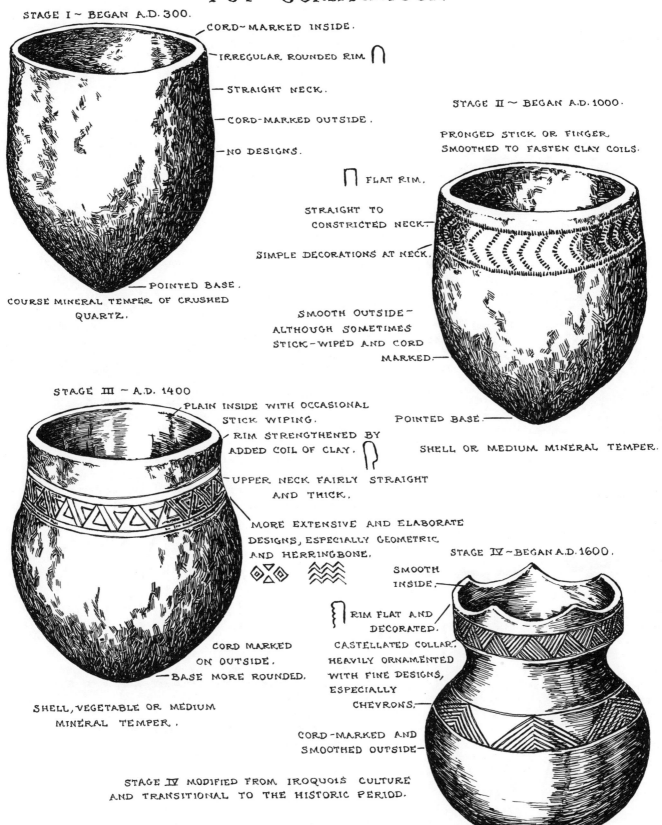

STAGE I ~ BEGAN A.D. 300.

CORD~MARKED INSIDE.

IRREGULAR ROUNDED RIM

STRAIGHT NECK.

CORD-MARKED OUTSIDE.

NO DESIGNS.

POINTED BASE.

COURSE MINERAL TEMPER OF CRUSHED QUARTZ.

STAGE II ~ BEGAN A.D. 1000.

PRONGED STICK OR FINGER SMOOTHED TO FASTEN CLAY COILS.

FLAT RIM.

STRAIGHT TO CONSTRICTED NECK.

SIMPLE DECORATIONS AT NECK.

SMOOTH OUTSIDE ~ ALTHOUGH SOMETIMES STICK~WIPED AND CORD MARKED.

POINTED BASE.

SHELL OR MEDIUM MINERAL TEMPER.

STAGE III ~ A.D. 1400

PLAIN INSIDE WITH OCCASIONAL STICK WIPING.

RIM STRENGTHENED BY ADDED COIL OF CLAY.

UPPER NECK FAIRLY STRAIGHT AND THICK.

MORE EXTENSIVE AND ELABORATE DESIGNS, ESPECIALLY GEOMETRIC AND HERRINGBONE.

CORD MARKED ON OUTSIDE.

BASE MORE ROUNDED.

SHELL, VEGETABLE OR MEDIUM MINERAL TEMPER.

STAGE IV ~ BEGAN A.D. 1600.

SMOOTH INSIDE.

RIM FLAT AND DECORATED.

CASTELLATED COLLAR.

HEAVILY ORNAMENTED WITH FINE DESIGNS, ESPECIALLY CHEVRONS.

CORD-MARKED AND SMOOTHED OUTSIDE.

STAGE IV MODIFIED FROM IROQUOIS CULTURE AND TRANSITIONAL TO THE HISTORIC PERIOD.

SEMI-ROUNDED BASE.

FINE MINERAL SHELL AND VEGETABLE TEMPER USED INTERCHANGEABLY.

41

POTS IN USE ~

EARLIER POINTED POTS
RESTED IN THE GROUND
WITH THE FIRE BUILT
AROUND THE BASE.

LATER CONSTRICTED NECKS
PERMITTED SUSPENSION OF
THE POT WITH THONGS.
THE GLOBULAR BASE EXPOSED A GREATER SURFACE TO THE HEAT.

SHELTER ~

The Algonquin of the Ceramic~Woodland period moved with the seasons. With the snows and cutting winds of winter, he preferred the protection of inland mountains and the deep forests. But spring meant planting down in the fertile valleys and fishing and shellfish hunting along the seacoast. New England's first mobile homes came into being ~ easily dismantled, backpacked and set up again. Only the matting or bark covering need be brought. The old sapling framework would still be standing from last year's trek ~ or could be cut handily at the campsite.

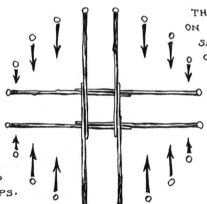

THE HUSBAND FIRST MARKED OUT A CIRCLE
ON THE GROUND, 10 TO 16 FEET IN DIAMETER.
SAPLINGS WERE EMBEDDED AROUND THE
CIRCUMFERENCE, EVERY 2 OR 3 FEET
APART.

OPPOSITE SAPLINGS
WERE BENT AND LASHED
WITH TOUGH BARK STRIPS.

TWO SETS OF OPPOSITE SAPLINGS
STARTED THE FRAME ~ NORTH TO SOUTH,
EAST TO WEST.

THE HIGHEST POINT IN THE
ARCH FRAMEWORK WAS 6 TO 8 FEET
HIGH.

HORIZONTAL SAPLINGS
SECURED THE
UPRIGHTS.

TWO ENTRANCES
WERE MADE AT THE
NORTH AND SOUTH
SIDES, EACH ABOUT
3 FEET IN
HEIGHT.

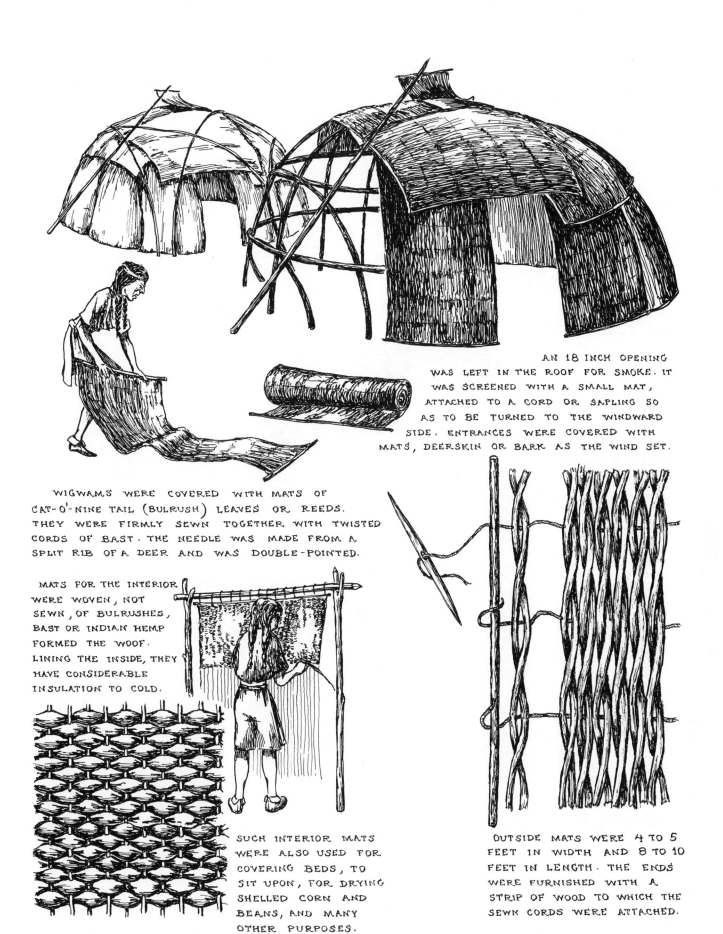

AN 18 INCH OPENING WAS LEFT IN THE ROOF FOR SMOKE. IT WAS SCREENED WITH A SMALL MAT, ATTACHED TO A CORD OR SAPLING SO AS TO BE TURNED TO THE WINDWARD SIDE. ENTRANCES WERE COVERED WITH MATS, DEERSKIN OR BARK AS THE WIND SET.

WIGWAMS WERE COVERED WITH MATS OF CAT-O'-NINE TAIL (BULRUSH) LEAVES OR REEDS. THEY WERE FIRMLY SEWN TOGETHER WITH TWISTED CORDS OF BAST. THE NEEDLE WAS MADE FROM A SPLIT RIB OF A DEER AND WAS DOUBLE-POINTED.

MATS FOR THE INTERIOR WERE WOVEN, NOT SEWN, OF BULRUSHES, BAST OR INDIAN HEMP FORMED THE WOOF. LINING THE INSIDE, THEY HAVE CONSIDERABLE INSULATION TO COLD.

SUCH INTERIOR MATS WERE ALSO USED FOR COVERING BEDS, TO SIT UPON, FOR DRYING SHELLED CORN AND BEANS, AND MANY OTHER PURPOSES.

OUTSIDE MATS WERE 4 TO 5 FEET IN WIDTH AND 8 TO 10 FEET IN LENGTH. THE ENDS WERE FURNISHED WITH A STRIP OF WOOD TO WHICH THE SEWN CORDS WERE ATTACHED.

("BAST" = INDIAN HEMP, LINDEN, SLIPPERY ELM OR SOME SUCH TREE HAVING FINE INNER BARK FOR SEWING.)

43

THESE SNUG DOMED WIGWAMS HELD ONE OR TWO FAMILIES INSIDE, THE FLOOR WAS OF TAMPED EARTH. SOME SLEPT ON MATS OR SKINS ON THE GROUND, BUT IN BETTER LODGES, PLATFORMS RINGED THE SIDES. THESE WERE BOTH SITTING AND SLEEPING PLACES, AND MADE BY SETTING FORKED STICKS INTO THE GROUND. THESE LEGS SUPPORTED HORIZONTAL POLES ABOUT 12 TO 18 INCHES ABOVE THE GROUND. STICKS RAN FROM THE FRONT POLE TO THE WIGWAM FRAME WHERE THEY WERE SECURED. IN THE LARGER HOUSES, THE BEDS WERE 6 TO 8 FEET WIDE, BROAD ENOUGH FOR 3 OR 4 PERSONS. THE BED FRAMEWORK WAS COVERED WITH BEDDING OF MATS AND SKINS.

WILLOUGHBY NOTED THAT THE HEARTHS WERE OFTEN OF SMALL FIELD STONES. SOMETIMES A POST RAN FROM BESIDE THE FIREPLACE TO A CROSS PIECE NEAR THE SMOKE HOLE. A STONE AT THE BASE PREVENTED SCORCHING. KETTLES COULD BE HUNG FROM PINS EXTENDING FROM THE POLE. OFTEN A FRAMEWORK OF GREEN STICKS, ABOUT TWO FEET ABOVE THE HEARTH, DRIED AND SMOKED FISH AND OTHER FOODS. TO THE ENGLISHMEN, IT WAS A DARK, SMOKY AND EVIL-SMELLING INTERIOR. THE WIGWAM HELD ONE OR TWO FAMILIES QUITE COMFORTABLY.

LONG HOUSES —

These large dwellings were used more frequently in winter. The smaller long houses had two smoke holes and sheltered four families. Three, four or more smoke holes housed six, eight or more families. Ceremonial houses were larger — sometimes one hundred or two hundred feet in length and thirty feet broad. A fifty foot long house could hold forty tribesmen comfortably.

There were two or more entrances, according to size. As with the smaller domed wigwams, they were covered with a deerskin or a mat. The better sort of long house was covered with bark. The early Europeans found these houses as warm and snug as their framed buildings.

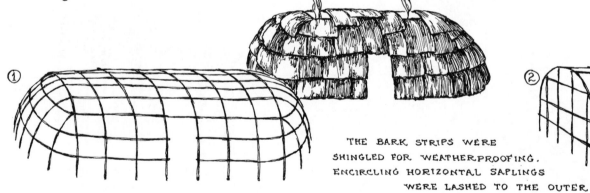

THE BARK STRIPS WERE SHINGLED FOR WEATHERPROOFING. ENCIRCLING HORIZONTAL SAPLINGS WERE LASHED TO THE OUTER SURFACE TO ANCHOR THE SHINGLES.

THE FRAMEWORK BEGAN WITH THE SETTING OF THE SAPLINGS IN TWO PARALLEL ROWS. OPPOSITE POLES WERE BENT AND LASHED TO EACH OTHER. THE ENDS WERE FORMED IN TWO WAYS:

① THE POLES WERE SET IN A SEMI-CIRCLE AND BENT TO JOIN THE MAIN FRAMEWORK.

② THE POLES WERE SET IN A STRAIGHT LINE, JOINING THE END ARCHES.

44

CONICAL WIGWAM –

In northern New England, especially in Abnaki country, the cone-shaped dwelling was in use. They resemble the skin-covered tipi of the western tribes.

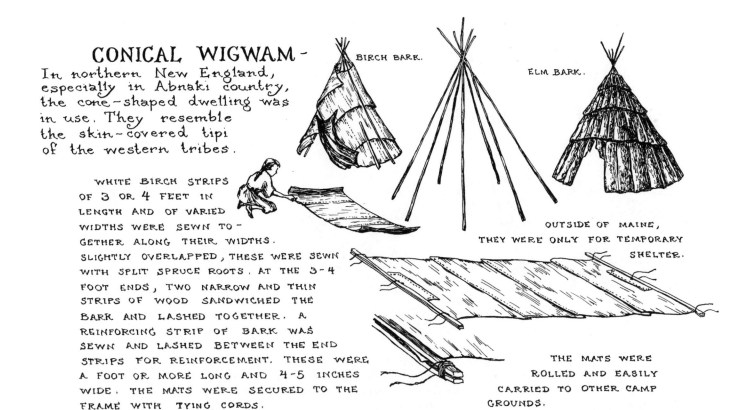

BIRCH BARK.

ELM BARK.

WHITE BIRCH STRIPS OF 3 OR 4 FEET IN LENGTH AND OF VARIED WIDTHS WERE SEWN TO-GETHER ALONG THEIR WIDTHS. SLIGHTLY OVERLAPPED, THESE WERE SEWN WITH SPLIT SPRUCE ROOTS. AT THE 3-4 FOOT ENDS, TWO NARROW AND THIN STRIPS OF WOOD SANDWICHED THE BARK AND LASHED TOGETHER. A REINFORCING STRIP OF BARK WAS SEWN AND LASHED BETWEEN THE END STRIPS FOR REINFORCEMENT. THESE WERE A FOOT OR MORE LONG AND 4-5 INCHES WIDE. THE MATS WERE SECURED TO THE FRAME WITH TYING CORDS.

OUTSIDE OF MAINE, THEY WERE ONLY FOR TEMPORARY SHELTER.

THE MATS WERE ROLLED AND EASILY CARRIED TO OTHER CAMP GROUNDS.

VILLAGES ~
Game, seafood, fertile fields and the availability of firewood determined the general location of the Algonquin village. Sites by ponds, rivers or along the coastline were usual. If any of these needs were lacking, or if the coming of winter required the protection of large hills as a windbreak, the villagers would move on. It required but a few hours to roll the mat covers and take to the trail. All that remained were the lonesome sap-ling skeletons of the wigwams, and perhaps a handful of those too ill or aged to go along on moving day.

The average village sheltered up to one hundred tribespeople. The wigwams were clustered about an open center space. Here the men and boys gathered for their games and ceremonies. There was more time for leisure since the men of the tribe had given over many of the old Indian crafts to the squaw. The women, in turn, bent their backs in the gardens that surrounded the living quarters. In short, village living was structured around the changing life styles of both men and women.

FORTIFIED VILLAGES ~

An unprotected village and its fertile fields were fair game for any less fortunate neighbors. It made good sense to protect one's hunting lands and gardens with some sort of barrier. The stockade answered that need. Willoughby estimated about twenty such forts, called "castles," were mentioned by the early explorers and colonists of New England between the years of 1605 and 1676.

Stockades surrounded the more permanent villages. The landscape was also used to advantage for defense. A favored location might be on the crest of a hill, on dry ground, and a commanding view of the countryside. If it were surrounded by a swamp, so much the better.

The palisade itself was of young trees, each about as thick as a man's thigh or the calf of his leg. Each was ten to twelve feet above the ground and three feet below the surface. Each was butted against its neighbor. An occasional crooked log was no disadvantage. Any gaps could be used as loopholes for shooting arrows.

The smaller stockades might be fifty feet in diameter and could surround a single wigwam or long house. It would have but one entrance. Larger forts would enclose a score or more wigwams. Two entrances would be usual ~ one on each side with overlapping ends. They could be filled with a tangle of brush at night or when an attack seemed likely. Both round and square stockades were in use.

The largest fort of King Philip's War (1675~1676) was located in Narragansett country. The Great Swamp at Kingston, Rhode Island, held a fort of about five hundred wigwams. The palisade was a feat of engineering. It enclosed four to five acres, and surrounding its base was a tangle of brush and trees to discourage attack.

THE COUNTRYSIDE ~ Thomas Morton, the happy~go~
lucky trader of Merry Mount, Massachusetts, knew his Algonquin neighbors well. In the 1620's he observed:

"The Salvages are accustomed to set fire of the Country in all places where they come, and to burn it twice a yeare, viz: at the Spring, and in the fall of the leafe. The reason that

moves them to doe so, is because it would other wise be so over-
growne with underweeds that it would be all a coppice wood, and
the people would not be able in any wise to passe through the Country
out of a beaten path ..... the burning of the grasse destroyes the
underwoods, and so scorcheth the elder trees that it shrinkes them,
and hinders their grouth very much: so that hee that will looke to
finde large trees and good tymber must not depend upon the help of
a wooden prospect to find them on the upland ground, but must
seeke for them (as I and others have done) in the lower grounds,
where the grounds are wett .... for the Salvages, by this custome
of theirs, have spoiled all the rest: for this custonme hath been
continued from the beginninge ....And this custome of firing the
country is the meanes to make it passable; and by that meanes
the trees growe here and there as in our parks: and makes the
Country very beautiful land commodious."

TRIBAL ORGANIZATION -

The loose-knit, happy and easy-going days of the Late Archaic
peoples were over. Perhaps the Adena people from Ohio introduced
their highly developed social levels to New England. Certainly some
sort of organization was necessary as the Algonquins of the Ceramic-
Woodland period increased their population and wealth.

The FAMILY was the basic unit of Indian
life. The father, as head of the family, had
the last word on any decision-making. Generally,
he had but one wife (two or more were not
uncommon for the sachem and men of wealth
and distinction). In spite of her newfound skills
with clay and planting, she was considered
man's inferior.
Both father and mother treated
their children with the greatest of
affection. When a child did a wrong,
his parents reasoned over the
problem with him and guided
him to better behavior. A wallop
on the backside was a real
rarity. Children were en-
couraged to be bold and
independent spirits at an
early age. They were free
to explore and sample the
world about them.

A CLAN or GENS was a
number of elite families having blood   ties or membership by
adoption. Clan members were descended through a female line,
while those in the gens were from a male line. These family
relations had their own special sections in the village. Each was
distinguished by a symbolic totem such as the bear, wolf or
tortoise. Since members of a clan or gens were considered
brothers or sisters, intermarriage was forbidden. An insult or
injury to one was considered an affront to all, and the warriors
of a clan or gens would take to the warpath together. At the

47

WOLF CLAN.

BEAR CLAN.

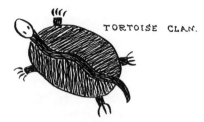
TORTOISE CLAN.

head of either group was a subchief, ready to give council and advice to his followers.

CLASSES~ 1. Nobles belonged to the highest class. Most exalted were those with royal blood lines, including the sachem of the tribe, members of a clan, or those adopted into a clan were lesser nobles. From this group came the subchiefs, shamans and other tribal officers. Their ranks supplied the sachem with his council of advisors.
    2. Sannops were the common people of the tribe and made up the bulk of the community. They possessed rights to the tribal lands and could accompany the sachem on his various excursions.
    3. Outsiders who had joined the tribe, as well as their descendants, made up the lowest class. They were little better than slaves, and in fact often acted as servants to the two upper classes. They had no legal rights, could own no land, and could not attend the sachem without permission. They scratched out their existence as best they could.

TRIBES were made up of a number of villages, each with their three classes of nobles, sannops and the lowly. The tribe occupied a definite territory and was an independent state.

The CHIEF SACHEM, holding office in one of the larger stockaded villages, ruled his tribe according to custom and tradition. His decisions were absolute by virtue of his royal ancestry. Talent, courage, or popularity had nothing to do with it. Because of his inherited power, later European settlers gave him the name of "king."
    If the sachem had no sons, his title was passed on to his wife, or "queen." If he was without wife, the title would descend to the next male in the blood line. Lacking a male heir, the next female became sachem. At all costs, royal blood must be kept pure.
    The sachem sat in judgement of wrongdoers, and personally saw to the punishment of the guilty. If one tribesman took the life of another, he would have the offender seized. Justice was dispatched quickly with a blow to the skull or a stab through the heart. If the killer had fled a considerable distance, he would send one of his councillors with his own warclub, tomahawk or knife as a warrant for the execution. For lesser evils, such as thievery, the sachem might hand him a public reprimand. A second offense would deserve a heavy thrashing. A third might have his nostrils slit, branding the thief so that all might thereafter be on their

48

guard when he was about.

TRIBAL COUNCIL ~ For weightier decisions, the sachem called into council a group of advisors. These were the lesser chieftains of the "noble" class, and known to the settlers of the Historic period as "sagamores." These men were distinguished for their leadership, warlike deeds or wisdom. Each had his own band of admirers and followers ~ the number depending on his popularity among the tribesmen. These lesser sachems had no power over these followers ~ quite the opposite of the chief sachem. Followers could leave the lesser sachem for another rival any time they wished.

The sachem and his council often formed an alliance with neighboring tribes against a common enemy. Such a union was known as a confederacy. This bond between tribes was more or less permanent.

A BAND was a group of families of a given tribe brought together temporarily. The band often formed a village which might or might not be made up of a single clan or gens group.

WAR!

Such organization was essential for preservation. The family or village that stood alone was fair game for any envious neighbor. Banding together under tribal leaders gave the advantage of both defensive and offensive warfare.

The stone bowl craftsman of the past became the Algonquin warrior ~ defender of his people and their way of life. The youngsters of the tribe were well aware of this role they must play. The glories of battle were frequently described by their elders. Games emphasized such admired qualities of the warrior as daring, self-reliance, agility, strength and endurance. The center field of the village became a proving ground for future war parties. Spectators turned out to cheer on games of stick-ball, stone throwing, weight lifting, running matches, wrestling, spirited dancing and marksmanship.

Although young men were allowed to watch the war dance, they could take no part until the age of sixteen. But every boy approaching manhood must first show his maturity through self reliance. Blind-folded, he was led into the wilderness in the dead of winter. There he must survive, armed only with a bow and arrows, a hatchet and a knife. During those solitary months, he must also choose his personal spirit guardian or manito. By spring he was returned to the village. His appearance would tell of his success or failure - and just how ready he was to join his fellows on the warpath.

A minor provocation could trigger a war dance. Insults were sure fuel for the war fires. A sachem who spoke contemptuously of another chieftain's ancestors could bring armed retaliation. Members of a family or clan were quick to defend the honor of any who had been ridiculed or suffered at the hands of an enemy. Previous raids were avenged by the victimized tribe. Cruelty and lust for killing had nothing to do with it. Any return attack was a warning to the enemy that their strength and determination were not to be taken lightly. Whole villages were massacred as the self-destruction of the Algonquin people mounted in fury. Victory never seemed to bring peace.

WAR DANCE

~ The night before taking to the war path, large fires silhouetted the throng of expectant villagers. A ripple of excitement ran through the village clearing as each fiercely painted warrior joined them. Then a hush fell as the war captain rose to his feet. He would be well-known and admired ~ a leader likely to bring off the raid successfully. If the war party were large, the sachem himself might lead. Smaller parties would be headed by the inferior chieftains.

His speech to the crowd was critical, for any who joined the war party were strictly volunteers. His appeal was certain to underline the fact that the forth-coming strike was with the approval and guidance of the Great Spirit. He had learned of this secret through a dream or some such contact. He would recount the evils perpetrated by the enemy and how these wrongs would be changed by revengeful braves under his leadership.

A drum began its slow pulse-rated beat. The war leader took up his club, smeared with vermilion to symbolize blood. The measured beat continued, now accompanied by a rattle and the songs of one or more warriors. The leader stamped the ground as if to shake the universe. His dance was highly figurative, involving the working of the clouds, carnivorous birds on the wing, and the influence of the spirits upon him. He heard a spirit voice from the cloud, and reached to take hold of the "circle in the sky" with his hands. As he danced about a painted post, he sang brief songs of heroic exploits and military deeds that would excite his audience. Every few moments he would raise his club in a threatening manner, strike furiously at the post, and go through the motions of dispatching his enemy.

Every warrior who rose and joined the war

dance became a volunteer. By so enlisting himself, the warrior could not honorably withdraw. Each in turn chanted his war song, told of his prowess on the battlefield, and mocked the cowardice of the foe. Each would boast of the warriors who would fall before his war club and of the women captives taken. His war cry would be answered by the spectators, now worked up to a fever pitch.

BATTLE FEVER ~
Indian fighting followed certain traditions. One such required an attacking tribe to forewarn the enemy. A mark or perhaps arrows might be planted near the target village that night, or a sheaf of arrows sent ahead (Cononicus, the Narragansett chief, did so with the Pilgrims). Sometimes lesser chiefs were dispatched to the enemy. They would review the insults and injuries suffered by his tribe and demand satisfaction.

Before taking to the trail or before the attack, the war party leaders usually gave a lengthy speech in an

WAR CLUBS ~ $\frac{1}{2}$ X

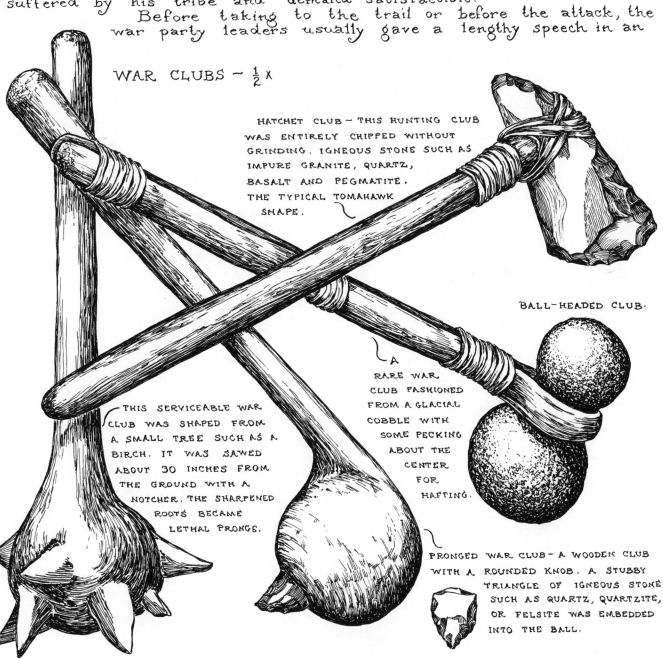

HATCHET CLUB ~ THIS HUNTING CLUB WAS ENTIRELY CHIPPED WITHOUT GRINDING. IGNEOUS STONE SUCH AS IMPURE GRANITE, QUARTZ, BASALT AND PEGMATITE. THE TYPICAL TOMAHAWK SHAPE.

BALL~HEADED CLUB.

A RARE WAR CLUB FASHIONED FROM A GLACIAL COBBLE WITH SOME PECKING ABOUT THE CENTER FOR HAFTING.

THIS SERVICEABLE WAR CLUB WAS SHAPED FROM A SMALL TREE SUCH AS A BIRCH. IT WAS SAWED ABOUT 30 INCHES FROM THE GROUND WITH A NOTCHER. THE SHARPENED ROOTS BECAME LETHAL PRONGS.

PRONGED WAR CLUB ~ A WOODEN CLUB WITH A ROUNDED KNOB. A STUBBY TRIANGLE OF IGNEOUS STONE SUCH AS QUARTZ, QUARTZITE, OR FELSITE WAS EMBEDDED INTO THE BALL.

51

effort to ridicule the enemy and praise the courage of his own warriors. Then the war party melted into the forest without a trace. By stepping from rock to rock or fallen tree, or passing down the course of a stream, no tell-tale footprints were left. When unavoidable, the party marched in a single file, stepping in the preceeding warrior's prints to conceal their numbers. Flankers probed ahead to prevent a surprise ambush. Warnings or signals were given by imitating woodland sounds - a wolf's howl, a loon's cry or some such - to avoid alerting an enemy within earshot.

Attacks on a village were rarely at night. The war party usually concealed themselves until daybreak when the enemy was in the deepest sleep. When the first dawn gave a measure of visability, the attack was begun. Generally the assault was poorly organized. It was every man for himself. Every advantage was taken of cover, but on open ground they would dodge and leap about to avoid the arrows. At the climax of the skirmish, the more aggressive of both parties would rush into hand to hand combat. Here the warrior could prove he had the qualities of bravery, daring and ruthlessness that were expected by his fellow tribesmen.

THE CAPTURED ~
Prisoners were occasionally adopted in place of a warrior slain in battle. Once accepted, he would take the place of the deceased, whether a son or a husband. He was considered as one of the tribe, although a wary eye was kept on him lest he attempt to leave his new relatives.

If a prisoner were not adopted, he faced death by torture. It was a slow and horrible way to meet one's maker. None the less, his past training in self control must help him to endure all the insults and torments that could be devised. At no time must he betray his agonies with an outcry or other signs of weakness. He must hurl back defiances, and as his last breath neared, he would taunt the enemy with his war song. Frequently, the women took a more active part than the men. To die in battle was considered the finest way for the warrior to end his life. But true greatness was granted he who could stand silent and immovable in the face of the torture.

WEAPONS ~ FOR BATTLE AND THE HUNT ~

SPEARS AND KNIVES ~

Spears were a rarity. Only war chiefs carried them - and sometimes using them as poles to carry back the heads of the chief enemies as trophies. Most spear-like points of the Ceramic ~ Woodland period were actually knives.

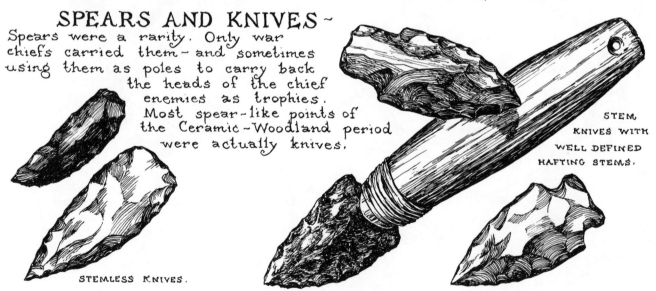

STEM KNIVES WITH WELL DEFINED HAFTING STEMS.

STEMLESS KNIVES.

ARROW POINTS ~
Many shapes and sizes filled the Ceramic~Woodland needs for hunting and warfare. The dark outlines highlight the individual point characteristics.

THIS GROUP WAS INHERITED FROM PAST CULTURES AND CONTINUED IN USE.

CORNER-REMOVED - FROM EARLY ARCHAIC.

SIDE-NOTCHED - LATE ARCHAIC.

DIAMOND - LATE ARCHAIC.

BASE WIDTH LESS THAN 1¼ INCHES.

SMALL TRIANGULAR FROM LATE ARCHAIC (PREVIOUSLY CURVED SIDES - NOW STRAIGHT.)

ALL ¾ X ±

THIS GROUP WAS DEVELOPED BY OR INTRODUCED TO THE CERAMIC~WOODLAND PEOPLE.

SIDE-NOTCHED -

LARGE TRIANGULAR - BASE WIDTH MORE THAN 1¼ INCHES.

CORNER-NOTCHED -

QUARTZ, QUARTZITE, FELSITE AND FLINT WERE PREFERRED FOR THESE POINTS.

HAFTING THE ARROW ~

COURSE GRAINED STONE.

½ X

NOTCHER - LATE ARCHAIC + CERAMIC.

ARROW SHAFTS WERE SLIGHTLY OVER THREE FEET IN LENGTH AND AND HALF AN INCH IN DIAMETER. A STRAIGHT HARDWOOD SAPLING WAS BENT TO STRETCH THE FIBERS, THEN SAWED WITH A STURDY NOTCHER.

½ X

SHAFT ABRADER. EARLY ARCHAIC - CERAMIC.

WITH THE BARK SKINNED FREE, A COURSE SHAFT SCRAPER SMOOTHED OUT KNOTS AND GAVE A GENTLE TAPER TOWARD THE FEATHER END.

BY HOLDING THE SHAFT STRAIGHT OVER HOT COALS, IT COULD BE WELL LINED AS THE OUTER FIBERS DRIED.

SHAFT ABRADERS - CERAMIC.

⅓ X

FINE GRAINED STONES WITH GROOVES OF ½ INCH ACROSS THESE STONES OF SANDSTONE, SCHIST OR ARGILLITE GAVE A FINAL SMOOTHING TO THE SHAFT WHEN THE WOOD DRIED.

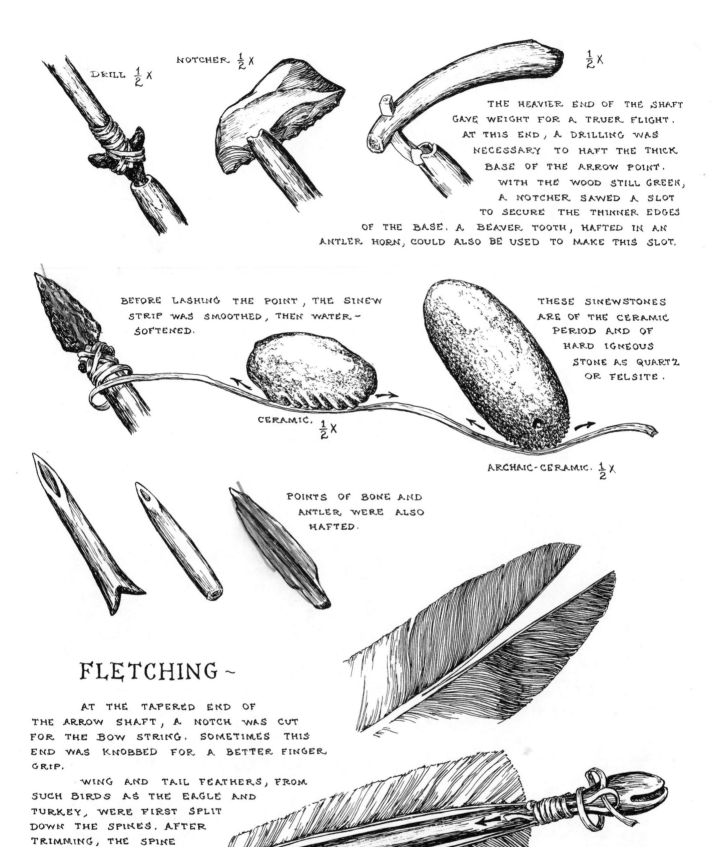

DRILL ½ X

NOTCHER ½ X

½ X

THE HEAVIER END OF THE SHAFT
GAVE WEIGHT FOR A TRUER FLIGHT.
AT THIS END, A DRILLING WAS
NECESSARY TO HAFT THE THICK
BASE OF THE ARROW POINT.
WITH THE WOOD STILL GREEN,
A NOTCHER SAWED A SLOT
TO SECURE THE THINNER EDGES
OF THE BASE. A BEAVER TOOTH, HAFTED IN AN
ANTLER HORN, COULD ALSO BE USED TO MAKE THIS SLOT.

BEFORE LASHING THE POINT, THE SINEW
STRIP WAS SMOOTHED, THEN WATER~
SOFTENED.

THESE SINEWSTONES
ARE OF THE CERAMIC
PERIOD AND OF
HARD IGNEOUS
STONE AS QUARTZ
OR FELSITE.

CERAMIC. ½ X

ARCHAIC-CERAMIC. ½ X

POINTS OF BONE AND
ANTLER WERE ALSO
HAFTED.

FLETCHING ~

AT THE TAPERED END OF
THE ARROW SHAFT, A NOTCH WAS CUT
FOR THE BOW STRING. SOMETIMES THIS
END WAS KNOBBED FOR A BETTER FINGER
GRIP.

WING AND TAIL FEATHERS, FROM
SUCH BIRDS AS THE EAGLE AND
TURKEY, WERE FIRST SPLIT
DOWN THE SPINES. AFTER
TRIMMING, THE SPINE
EXTENSIONS WERE
LASHED TO THE
SHAFT WITH
FINE GUT.

TWO OR THREE
FEATHERS WERE
LASHED TO THE
SHAFT.

BOWS~

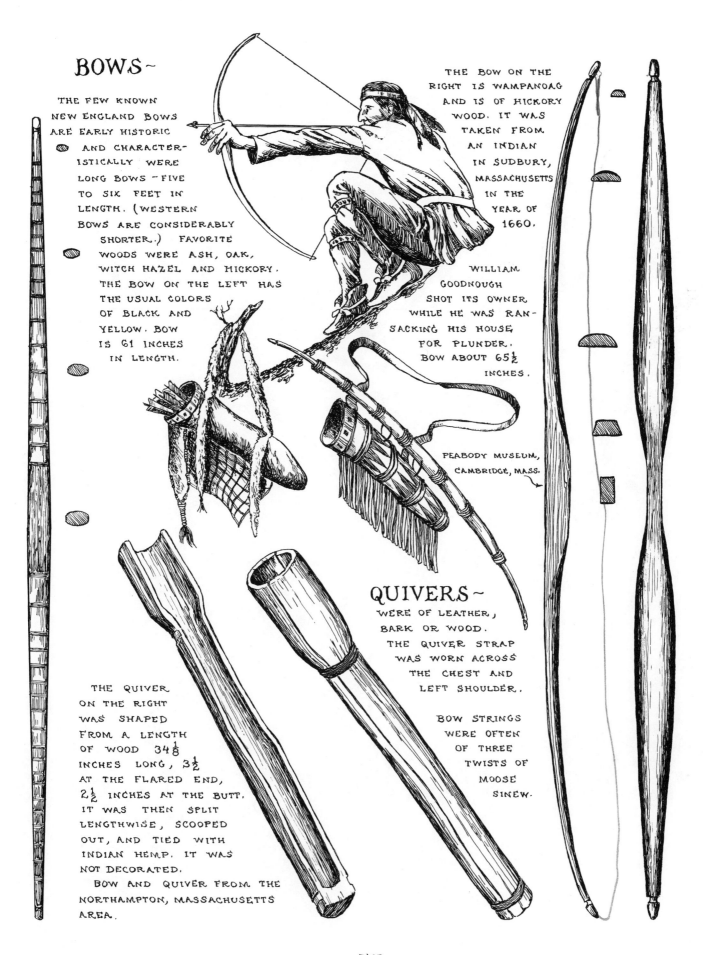

THE FEW KNOWN NEW ENGLAND BOWS ARE EARLY HISTORIC AND CHARACTERISTICALLY WERE LONG BOWS — FIVE TO SIX FEET IN LENGTH. (WESTERN BOWS ARE CONSIDERABLY SHORTER.) FAVORITE WOODS WERE ASH, OAK, WITCH HAZEL AND HICKORY. THE BOW ON THE LEFT HAS THE USUAL COLORS OF BLACK AND YELLOW. BOW IS 61 INCHES IN LENGTH.

THE BOW ON THE RIGHT IS WAMPANOAG AND IS OF HICKORY WOOD. IT WAS TAKEN FROM AN INDIAN IN SUDBURY, MASSACHUSETTS IN THE YEAR OF 1660.

WILLIAM GOODNOUGH SHOT ITS OWNER WHILE HE WAS RANSACKING HIS HOUSE FOR PLUNDER. BOW ABOUT 65½ INCHES.

PEABODY MUSEUM, CAMBRIDGE, MASS.

QUIVERS~

WERE OF LEATHER, BARK OR WOOD. THE QUIVER STRAP WAS WORN ACROSS THE CHEST AND LEFT SHOULDER.

BOW STRINGS WERE OFTEN OF THREE TWISTS OF MOOSE SINEW.

THE QUIVER ON THE RIGHT WAS SHAPED FROM A LENGTH OF WOOD 34⅛ INCHES LONG, 3½ AT THE FLARED END, 2½ INCHES AT THE BUTT. IT WAS THEN SPLIT LENGTHWISE, SCOOPED OUT, AND TIED WITH INDIAN HEMP. IT WAS NOT DECORATED.

BOW AND QUIVER FROM THE NORTHAMPTON, MASSACHUSETTS AREA.

HUNTING ~

THE DEADFALL.

THE SNARE.

The warrior took up his hunting weapons soon after harvest time was over. He tracked his quarry until he was snow-bound by winter. Rabbit, raccoon, squirrel, deer, moose and bear were regular contributors to the stew pot. Although otter and beaver were also eaten, fur was their chief value. Carnivorous animals ~ fox, wolf and wildcat ~ were not eaten at all, but their pelts were prized by the tribesmen. Wild fowl were also prime marks for the arrow ~ pigeon, quail, turkey, partridge, duck and geese.

The hunter was off at the first hint of dawn. Tracks were his road map ~ they told him the kind of critter, its speed, direction and how long ago it had passed that way. When stalking

TRAPPING WAS AN ART. A PROPERLY SET TRAP BROUGHT THE HUNTED TO THE HUNTER. SNARES COULD SNATCH UP ANY BIRD OR BEAST UP TO THE SIZE OF A DEER. IT WAS SALTED WITH SUCH AS ACORNS OR CORN. OR THERE WAS THE DEADLY DEADFALL, HEAVY ENOUGH TO FLATTEN A BEAR UNDER ITS WEIGHT.

uphill, the hunter melted into the shadow side of the rise, the better to see the adjacent sunlit hill-sides ~ and to hide himself from his quarry and any lurking enemy. At dusk he would make his way into the valley, for there the animals of the forest gathered at the end of the day.

The natural curiosity of the deer was its downfall. When startled, it would bound off, only to stop short and see what the disturbance was all about. The pause was usually within arrow range.

DEER DRIVES WERE A GROUP EFFORT. FENCES
A MILE OR TWO LONG WERE BUILT IN THE SHAPE OF
A GIGANTIC "V". AS TRIBESMEN DROVE THE DEER DOWN
THE FUNNEL, OTHERS WAITED IN AMBUSH AT THE APEX OPENING.
DURING THE NIGHT, SNARES WERE SET AT THE OPENING TO CATCH
STRAGGLERS.

The Indian dog survived and multiplied since the Archaic days. Early Europeans thought they were tame foxes or coyotes, but they remained the same primitive Asian dogs without benefit of cross~breeding with wild animals. They were kept as a reserve food supply to be eaten when game was scarce. In the meantime, they would rid the camp of mice and garbage - or sound a warning when hostile warriors approached. One thing seems certain - the Ceramic~Woodland hunter rarely used his dog for hunting or as a pet.

Rewards of the hunt yielded more than meat. From skin to bones, it seemed that the thrifty Indian had a use for everything.
Skin~ moccasins, thongs, clothing.
Hair ~ stiff hair from the tail made ornaments and embroidery.
Antlers - tools and arrow points.
Hoofs ~ rattles.
Dew claws ~ the vestigial leg digit not reaching the ground was
    used as jinglers for belts, anklets and rattles.
Sinews~ these strong tendons were dressed for thread, bow~
    strings and snares.
Bones ~ for bodkins (hairpins and needles), skin-dressing tools,
    handles and ornaments.
Bladders ~ bags and containers.
Meat~ preserved by cutting into strips and drying in the smoke.
    Moose tongue was a delicacy. Fresh meat was cooked on
    spits, supported by a pair of forked sticks.

SHELLFISH

~ Shell heaps along the New England coastline remain as monuments to the Ceramic-Woodland people's taste in shellfish. (Earlier cultures had never known the eating pleasure that waited between those calcified covers.) Anyone with the time and patience to sort over the shell residue would find the soft-shell clam making up ninety-five percent of the whole. Quahaugs, razor clams and mussels made up the bulk of the remainder. Scallops were a rare finding.

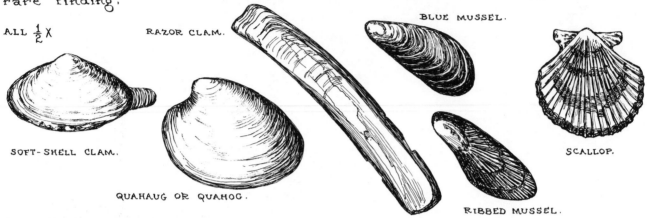

ALL ½ X

RAZOR CLAM.

BLUE MUSSEL.

SOFT-SHELL CLAM.

QUAHAUG OR QUAHOG.

RIBBED MUSSEL.

SCALLOP.

The shell heaps have also yielded a variety of associated tools.

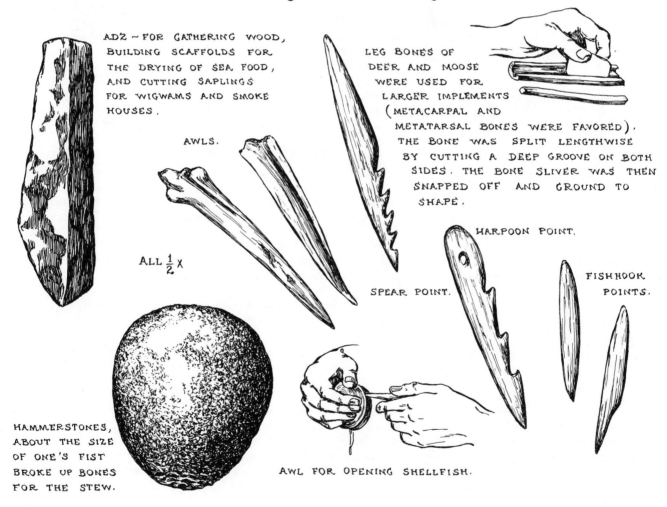

ADZ ~ FOR GATHERING WOOD, BUILDING SCAFFOLDS FOR THE DRYING OF SEA FOOD, AND CUTTING SAPLINGS FOR WIGWAMS AND SMOKE HOUSES.

AWLS.

ALL ½ X

HAMMERSTONES, ABOUT THE SIZE OF ONE'S FIST BROKE UP BONES FOR THE STEW.

AWL FOR OPENING SHELLFISH.

LEG BONES OF DEER AND MOOSE WERE USED FOR LARGER IMPLEMENTS (METACARPAL AND METATARSAL BONES WERE FAVORED). THE BONE WAS SPLIT LENGTHWISE BY CUTTING A DEEP GROOVE ON BOTH SIDES. THE BONE SLIVER WAS THEN SNAPPED OFF AND GROUND TO SHAPE.

SPEAR POINT.

HARPOON POINT.

FISHHOOK POINTS.

Further probing of the shell heaps has produced pointed sticks of various lengths, from three quarters of an inch to two and a half inches in diameter. It would seem likely that these saplings were driven into the sand and used as fire screens and wind-breaks. They would also be handy as supports for drying racks and the temporary framework for wigwams and smoke houses.

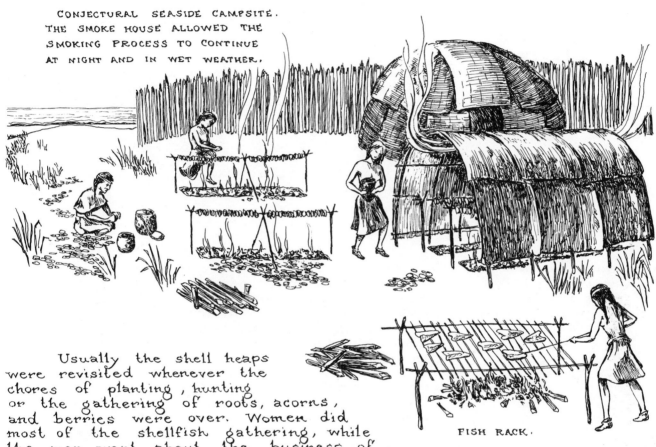

CONJECTURAL SEASIDE CAMPSITE. THE SMOKE HOUSE ALLOWED THE SMOKING PROCESS TO CONTINUE AT NIGHT AND IN WET WEATHER.

FISH RACK.

Usually the shell heaps were revisited whenever the chores of planting, hunting or the gathering of roots, acorns, and berries were over. Women did most of the shellfish gathering, while the men went about the business of fishing. Although clams and their relatives were dug at low tide, it could be a damp, chilly process in mid-winter.

Teams of squaws shucked the shellfish, then speared the meat on a long green stick. (A freshly cut branch would resist burning and should be of a sweet wood.) Lobster and eel meat were preserved the same way. The drying and smoking was accomplished without benefit of salt. As a matter of fact, salt was unknown as a seasoning. The broth of boiled clams and a thickened broth called "Nasaump" served well as a seasoning. It was considered especially tasty in the flavoring of breads.

Crabs were generally roasted in their shells. Fish were cut into chunks or split, then dried and smoked before rain or the flies could spoil the meat. Actually, the smoky fires did their bit to discourage the hungry pests. When the preservation process was over, the long stick supports made handy racks for carrying the seafood back to the inland camps.

59

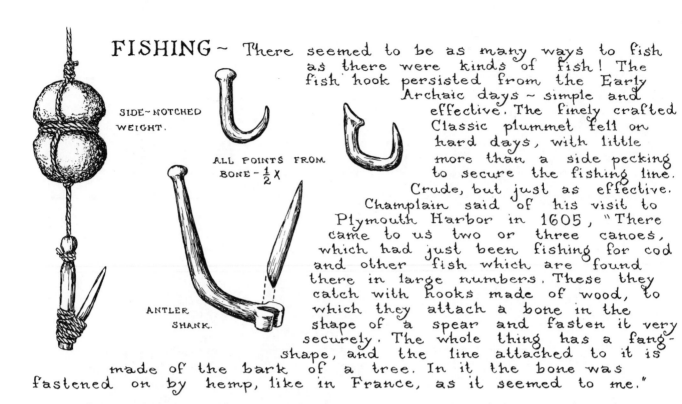

FISHING ~

There seemed to be as many ways to fish as there were kinds of fish! The fish hook persisted from the Early Archaic days ~ simple and effective. The finely crafted Classic plummet fell on hard days, with little more than a side pecking to secure the fishing line. Crude, but just as effective.

SIDE~NOTCHED WEIGHT.

ALL POINTS FROM BONE ~ 1/2 X

ANTLER SHANK.

Champlain said of his visit to Plymouth Harbor in 1605, "There came to us two or three canoes, which had just been fishing for cod and other fish which are found there in large numbers. These they catch with hooks made of wood, to which they attach a bone in the shape of a spear and fasten it very securely. The whole thing has a fang-shape, and the line attached to it is made of the bark of a tree. In it the bone was fastened on by hemp, like in France, as it seemed to me."

Spearing fish was popular. Even the youngsters tried their luck with sharpened sticks.

SPEAR POINTS OF BONE.

BONE HARPOON POINTS (THEY MUST HAVE A LINE HOLE TO BE USED AS A HARPOON) TOOK SUCH MEDIUM AND LARGE FISH AS SEA BASS, BLUEFISH, AND STURGEON. THEY WERE HUSKY ENOUGH TO BRING IN SEALS. THE POINT WAS WEDGED INTO THE SHAFT. A LONG LINE, SECURED TO THE DUG-OUT AND TO THE POINT, WAS USED TO HAUL OUT THE FISH WHEN IT WAS STRUCK AND THE POINT DISLODGED.

LOBSTERS WERE SPEARED WITH A STAFF 2 OR 3 YARDS LONG.

CANOES WENT OUT AT LOW TIDE WHEN THE WINDS STOOD STILL. THE LOBSTER WAS STUCK TOWARD THE HEAD AND LIFTED ABOARD.

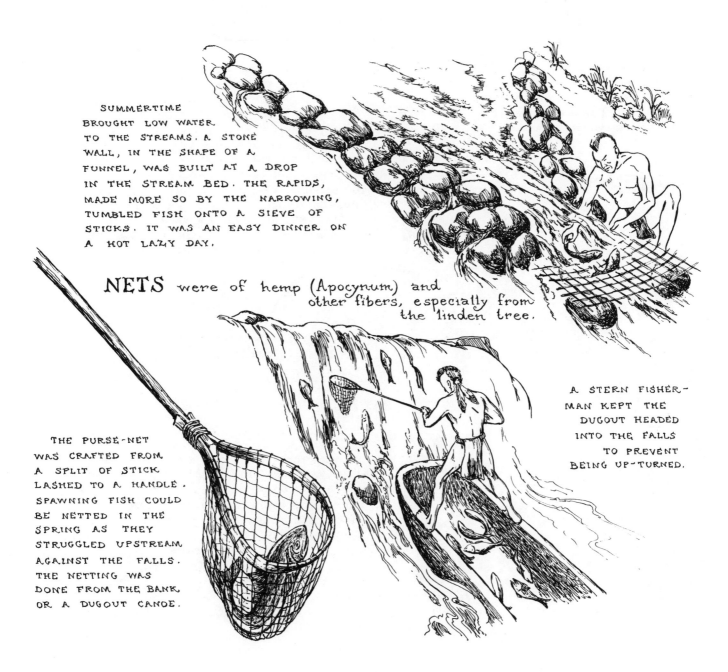

SPRING BROUGHT THE SPAWNING RUNS. AN ENTERPRISING INDIAN COULD FENCE OFF THE OUTLET OF A STREAM WITH BRANCHES. FISH WOULD HAVE NO TROUBLE SWIMMING THROUGH THE FENCE OPENING TO THE SPAWNING GROUNDS. BUT ON THE RETURN, THE CURRENT FORCED THEM AGAINST THE BRANCH BARRIER. BY SIGHT AND FEEL, THE FISHERMAN COULD HOOK HIS SPEAR PRONG UNDER THE FISH AND YANK IT TO THE SURFACE.

$\frac{1}{2}$ X
SIMPLE FISH SPEAR — BONE POINT.

SUMMERTIME BROUGHT LOW WATER TO THE STREAMS. A STONE WALL, IN THE SHAPE OF A FUNNEL, WAS BUILT AT A DROP IN THE STREAM BED. THE RAPIDS, MADE MORE SO BY THE NARROWING, TUMBLED FISH ONTO A SIEVE OF STICKS. IT WAS AN EASY DINNER ON A HOT LAZY DAY.

NETS were of hemp (Apocynum) and other fibers, especially from the linden tree.

THE PURSE-NET WAS CRAFTED FROM A SPLIT OF STICK LASHED TO A HANDLE. SPAWNING FISH COULD BE NETTED IN THE SPRING AS THEY STRUGGLED UPSTREAM AGAINST THE FALLS. THE NETTING WAS DONE FROM THE BANK OR A DUGOUT CANOE.

A STERN FISHER-MAN KEPT THE DUGOUT HEADED INTO THE FALLS TO PREVENT BEING UP-TURNED.

61

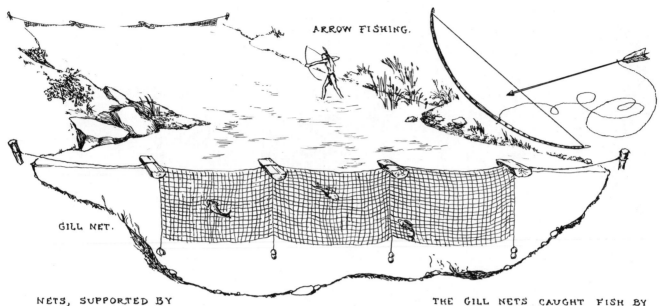

ARROW FISHING.

GILL NET.

NETS, SUPPORTED BY
FLOATS OF WOOD OR BARK, BLOCKED
OFF A COVE OR SALT WATER INLET.
WHEN THE TIDE LOWERED, FISH
COULD BE TAKEN WITH ARROWS.

THE GILL NETS CAUGHT FISH BY
THEIR GILLS IN THE HEMP SCREEN.
THE NETS WERE HELD DOWN WITH
THE SIDE-NOTCHED WEIGHTS.

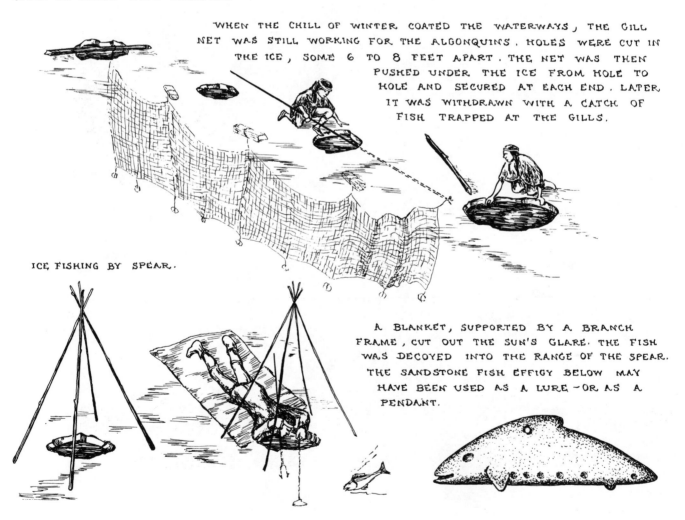

WHEN THE CHILL OF WINTER COATED THE WATERWAYS, THE GILL
NET WAS STILL WORKING FOR THE ALGONQUINS. HOLES WERE CUT IN
THE ICE, SOME 6 TO 8 FEET APART. THE NET WAS THEN
PUSHED UNDER THE ICE FROM HOLE TO
HOLE AND SECURED AT EACH END. LATER
IT WAS WITHDRAWN WITH A CATCH OF
FISH TRAPPED AT THE GILLS.

ICE FISHING BY SPEAR.

A BLANKET, SUPPORTED BY A BRANCH
FRAME, CUT OUT THE SUN'S GLARE. THE FISH
WAS DECOYED INTO THE RANGE OF THE SPEAR.
THE SANDSTONE FISH EFFIGY BELOW MAY
HAVE BEEN USED AS A LURE — OR AS A
PENDANT.

62

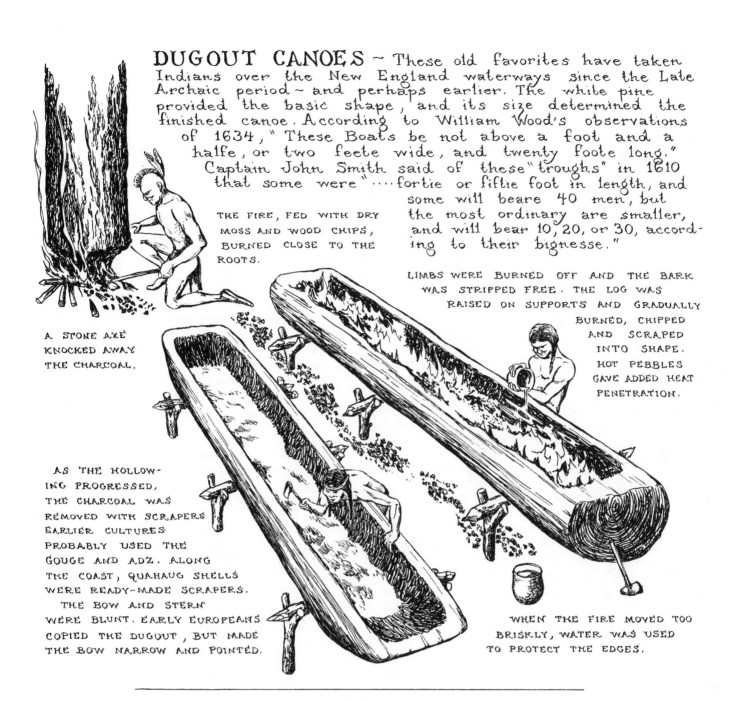

DUGOUT CANOES ~
These old favorites have taken Indians over the New England waterways since the Late Archaic period ~ and perhaps earlier. The white pine provided the basic shape, and its size determined the finished canoe. According to William Wood's observations of 1634, "These Boats be not above a foot and a halfe, or two feete wide, and twenty foote long." Captain John Smith said of these "troughs" in 1610 that some were "....fortie or fiftie foot in length, and some will beare 40 men, but the most ordinary are smaller, and will bear 10, 20, or 30, according to their bignesse."

THE FIRE, FED WITH DRY MOSS AND WOOD CHIPS, BURNED CLOSE TO THE ROOTS.

A STONE AXE KNOCKED AWAY THE CHARCOAL.

LIMBS WERE BURNED OFF AND THE BARK WAS STRIPPED FREE. THE LOG WAS RAISED ON SUPPORTS AND GRADUALLY BURNED, CHIPPED AND SCRAPED INTO SHAPE. HOT PEBBLES GAVE ADDED HEAT PENETRATION.

AS THE HOLLOWING PROGRESSED, THE CHARCOAL WAS REMOVED WITH SCRAPERS EARLIER CULTURES PROBABLY USED THE GOUGE AND ADZ. ALONG THE COAST, QUAHAUG SHELLS WERE READY-MADE SCRAPERS.

THE BOW AND STERN WERE BLUNT. EARLY EUROPEANS COPIED THE DUGOUT, BUT MADE THE BOW NARROW AND POINTED.

WHEN THE FIRE MOVED TOO BRISKLY, WATER WAS USED TO PROTECT THE EDGES.

500 YEARS AGO, THIS DUGOUT GAVE SERVICE IN THE WEYMOUTH, MASSACHUSETTS AREA. DISCOVERED IN 1965, IT HAD BEEN PRESERVED IN NEARBY GREAT POND, UNDER THE SLUDGE OF CENTURIES. ON DISPLAY AT THE TUFTS LIBRARY IN WEYMOUTH, THIS FINE SPECIMEN MEASURES ROUGHLY 11 FEET LONG, 2 FEET WIDE AND ABOUT 11 INCHES IN DEPTH.

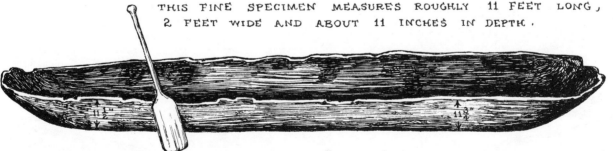

PADDLE DESCRIPTIONS ARE RARE INDEED. ONE A. L. de D. LAHONTAN DESCRIBED IN 1735 ONE OF MAPLE, HAVING A BLADE 20 INCHES LONG AND A HANDLE 3 FEET IN LENGTH.

BIRCH BARK CANOE ~ RAW MATERIALS

FINE STANDS OF PAPER BIRCH (BETULA PAPYRIFERA MARSH.) IN NEW HAMPSHIRE AND MAINE WERE RIGHTLY KNOWN AS CANOE BIRCH. BARK FROM THESE GIANTS ~ SOME WERE 30 OR MORE INCHES IN DIAMETER ~ YIELDED THE BEST BARK DURING A WINTER THAW, EARLY SPRING OR LATE FALL TO PREVENT THE STRONG GREENISH-YELLOW INNER RIND ~ THE CAMBIUM LAYER ~ FROM SEPARATING.

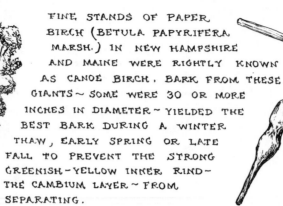

BLACK SPRUCE.

WATER ~ PROOFING.

NARROW STRIPS OF BARK WERE REMOVED FROM THE BLACK OR WHITE SPRUCE IN THE EARLY SPRING. RESIN COLLECTED AT THE BOTTOM OF THE SCAR DURING WARM WEATHER. AFTER MELTING IN A BOWL, IT WAS TEMPERED WITH ANIMAL FAT AND A LITTLE FINELY POWDERED CHARCOAL. A STRIP OF BARK WAS TESTED BY DIPPING INTO THE MIXTURE. MORE TEMPER WAS NEEDED IF IT CRACKED, BECAME TACKY, OR RUBBED OFF EASILY.

A LONGITUDINAL CUT WAS MADE WITH A STONE BLADE AND MALL OR WITH A SLASHING CUT WITH A STONE KNIFE. A CHISEL-SHAPED STICK PRIED AWAY THE BARK SHEET. IT WAS THEN ROLLED AND SUBMERGED TO KEEP PLIABLE.

SEWING WAS CHIEFLY WITH BLACK SPRUCE ROOT (PICEA MARIANA). EACH HAD CONSIDERABLE LENGTH AND SMALL DIAMETER. THE BARK WAS STRIPPED WITH A KNIFE, CLAMSHELL, OR PERHAPS THE THUMBNAIL. THE ROOT WAS SPLIT APART BY BITING, THEN SEPARATED DOWN ITS FULL LENGTH.

CONSTRUCTION ~

THE CANOE FRAME WAS OF WHITE CEDAR. STARTING AT THE SMALLER END, THE LOG WAS SPLIT INTO LENGTHS. AX OR KNIFE WEDGES WERE POUNDED ALONG THE SPLIT AS IT OPENED DOWN THE GRAIN.

TWO HOLES WERE DRILLED INTO THE GUNWALE, THEN SPLIT OUT WITH A BEAVER'S TOOTH CHISEL. THIS SLOT SECURED THE THWART AFTER BEING PEGGED.

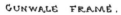

GUNWALE FRAME.

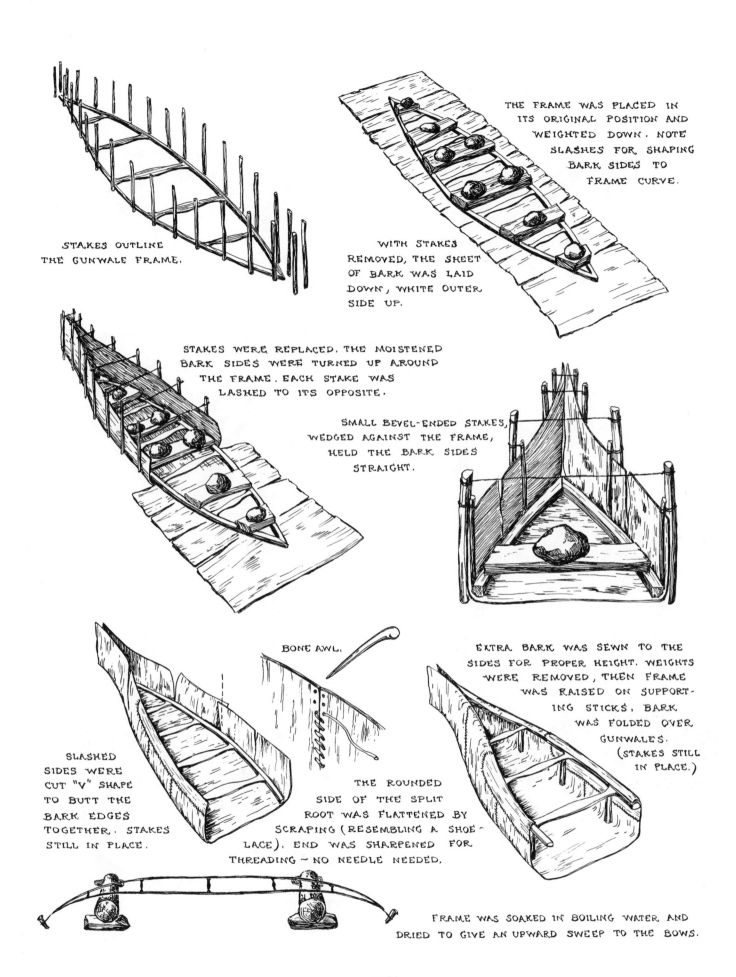

STAKES OUTLINE
THE GUNWALE FRAME.

THE FRAME WAS PLACED IN
ITS ORIGINAL POSITION AND
WEIGHTED DOWN. NOTE
SLASHES FOR SHAPING
BARK SIDES TO
FRAME CURVE.

WITH STAKES
REMOVED, THE SHEET
OF BARK WAS LAID
DOWN, WHITE OUTER
SIDE UP.

STAKES WERE REPLACED. THE MOISTENED
BARK SIDES WERE TURNED UP AROUND
THE FRAME. EACH STAKE WAS
LASHED TO ITS OPPOSITE.

SMALL BEVEL-ENDED STAKES,
WEDGED AGAINST THE FRAME,
HELD THE BARK SIDES
STRAIGHT.

BONE AWL.

EXTRA BARK WAS SEWN TO THE
SIDES FOR PROPER HEIGHT. WEIGHTS
WERE REMOVED, THEN FRAME
WAS RAISED ON SUPPORT-
ING STICKS. BARK
WAS FOLDED OVER
GUNWALES.
(STAKES STILL
IN PLACE.)

SLASHED
SIDES WERE
CUT "V" SHAPE
TO BUTT THE
BARK EDGES
TOGETHER. STAKES
STILL IN PLACE.

THE ROUNDED
SIDE OF THE SPLIT
ROOT WAS FLATTENED BY
SCRAPING (RESEMBLING A SHOE-
LACE). END WAS SHARPENED FOR
THREADING ~ NO NEEDLE NEEDED.

FRAME WAS SOAKED IN BOILING WATER AND
DRIED TO GIVE AN UPWARD SWEEP TO THE BOWS.

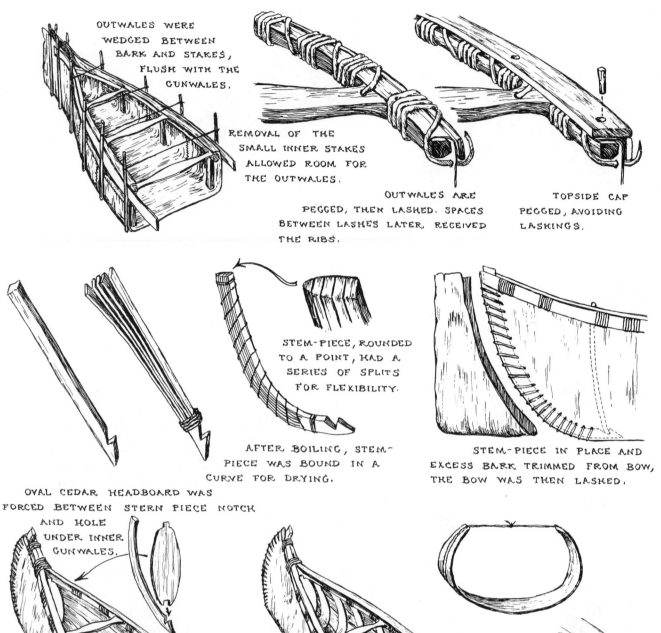

OUTWALES WERE WEDGED BETWEEN BARK AND STAKES, FLUSH WITH THE GUNWALES.

REMOVAL OF THE SMALL INNER STAKES ALLOWED ROOM FOR THE OUTWALES.

OUTWALES ARE PEGGED, THEN LASHED. SPACES BETWEEN LASHES LATER RECEIVED THE RIBS.

TOPSIDE CAP PEGGED, AVOIDING LASHINGS.

STEM-PIECE, ROUNDED TO A POINT, HAD A SERIES OF SPLITS FOR FLEXIBILITY.

AFTER BOILING, STEM-PIECE WAS BOUND IN A CURVE FOR DRYING.

STEM-PIECE IN PLACE AND EXCESS BARK TRIMMED FROM BOW, THE BOW WAS THEN LASHED.

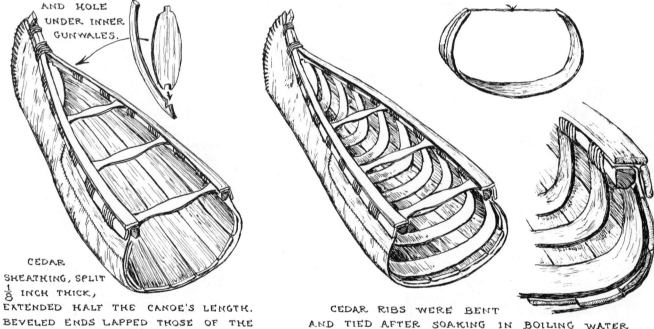

OVAL CEDAR HEADBOARD WAS FORCED BETWEEN STERN PIECE NOTCH AND HOLE UNDER INNER GUNWALES.

CEDAR SHEATHING, SPLIT $\frac{1}{8}$ INCH THICK, EXTENDED HALF THE CANOE'S LENGTH. BEVELED ENDS LAPPED THOSE OF THE REMAINING HALF. BARK WAS SOAKED TO ROUND THE BOTTOM.

CEDAR RIBS WERE BENT AND TIED AFTER SOAKING IN BOILING WATER WHEN DRY, EACH WAS CUT TO SIZE AND FORCED INTO THE BEVEL UNDER THE INNER GUNWALE.

66

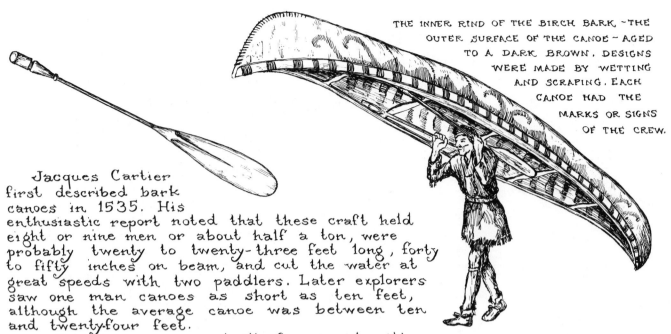

THE INNER RIND OF THE BIRCH BARK ~ THE OUTER SURFACE OF THE CANOE ~ AGED TO A DARK BROWN. DESIGNS WERE MADE BY WETTING AND SCRAPING. EACH CANOE HAD THE MARKS OR SIGNS OF THE CREW.

Jacques Cartier first described bark canoes in 1535. His enthusiastic report noted that these craft held eight or nine men or about half a ton, were probably twenty to twenty-three feet long, forty to fifty inches on beam, and cut the water at great speeds with two paddlers. Later explorers saw one man canoes as short as ten feet, although the average canoe was between ten and twenty-four feet.

War canoes were built for speed with sharp ends and a narrow beam. Most were not over eighteen feet in length ~ just large enough for three or four warriors. However, the Iroquois boasted of a canoe that could cruise the Great Lakes with over fifty braves!

Little wonder that the Europeans were so taken with this work of the northern Indian craftsmen! Swift on the water, it could be easily managed by a single paddler. It could carry great loads, but was light enough for a one man carry. Raw materials for repair were everywhere. It was sturdy and waterproof, and when weighted with stones and sunk, the canoe would be ready for use after months of submersion.

WOODEN CONTAINERS ~

The dugout canoe had a small relative, crafted to keep fluids in rather than out. Wooden spoons and bowls were fashioned from tree burls. As with the dugout, they were painstakingly charred and scraped to a thin shell. Each had a handle ~ straight up and flat ~ while some of the larger serving bowls boasted of two handles. Since soups and mushy concoctions simmered in every wigwam pot, those spoons, cups, scoops and bowls were owned and used by practically everyone. In spite of the numbers in use, only an occasional wooden container has survived destruction in New England's soil.

THIS SHALLOW SPOON WAS FOUND IN AN ONTARIO COUNTY GRAVE, N.Y. ~ (SIMILAR TO NEW ENGLAND'S.)

½ X

½ X

RARE 7 INCH BOWL FROM A CONNECTICUT VALLEY BURIAL. A CRACK WAS REPAIRED WITH A LASHING THROUGH TWO DRILLED HOLES.

67

PIPES ~

Smoking continued to gain favor since the soapstone pipe days. The women turned their skills toward making a variety of clay pipes, but left the smoking to the men. And the male considered it his privilege to grow the tobacco — but there he drew the line with the back-bending business of gardening.

Stage I (to 1000 A.D.) — The Straight pipe.

THIS FIRST AND LEAST POPULAR PIPE WAS MADE BY FIRST INDENTING THE BOWL WITH A FINGER, THEN PUSHING A STICK THROUGH TO MEET THE CAVITY. THIS COULD BE LEFT IN PLACE AND THE CHAR REMOVED AFTER FIRING. THE STEM HOLES OF LATER PIPES WERE MADE IN THE SAME WAY. CRUSHED SHELLS OR STONE TEMPERED THE CLAY.

3/4 X

Stage II and III (1000 A.D. to 1600 A.D.) ~ The Elbow pipe.

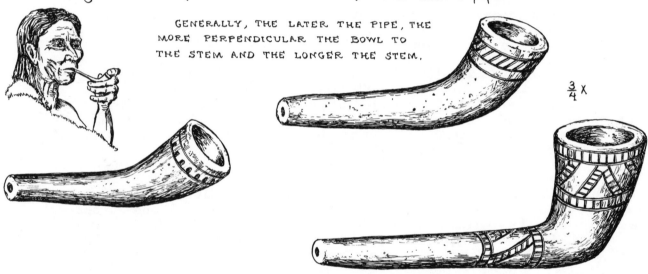

GENERALLY, THE LATER THE PIPE, THE MORE PERPENDICULAR THE BOWL TO THE STEM AND THE LONGER THE STEM.

3/4 X

Stage IV (1600 to 1650 A.D.) ~ Elbow trumpet.

AS WITH THE STAGE IV POTS, THE COLLARS SHOW A STRONG IROQUOIS INFLUENCE.

ALTHOUGH TRANSITIONAL INTO THE HISTORICAL PERIOD, THE STYLE WAS NOT INFLUENCED BY THE EUROPEANS.

3/4 X

3/4 X

RELIGION~

CHIEF GOD ~

When the earth was young, evil spirits unleashed a devastating flood. Some animals escaped a watery death by fleeing to the great mountain in the southwest. There lived the great and good god Cautantowit ~ also known to various Algonquin tribes as Kiehtan or Woonand. Protected in this mountaintop house, those birds and beasts of the forest had many god-like qualities because of the close association with Him.

MAIZE EAR, MAINE.

After remaking the mud-soaked earth, Cautantowit set about to fashion a man and woman from stone. Dissatisfied with the results, He smashed them into fragments. Again He created a man and a woman, this time from a living tree. He was pleased. Through His handiwork, these humans and their kin possessed immortal souls. He then gave His people general guidelines for living, and corn and beans from His garden. If the Algonquin had made the most of his god-given gifts ~ wisdom, valor, strength, activity and the like ~ his soul after death could journey to the great southwest house of Cautantowit. There he would live in peace and plenty. On the other hand, murderers, thieves and liars were doomed to a restless wandering throughout eternity.

SNAKE AMULET~ NARRAGANSETT BAY.

LESSER GODS ~

Yet Cautantowit never meddled in the worldly affairs of His subjects. On earth, guidance, hope, comfort and fortitude came from the spirits of the birds, beasts and fish. A bit of God was in them from their early refuge to the southwest. Each Algonquin chose one such personal god or manito as his guardian. At times this spirit would reveal itself to its ward through dreams, visions or the mysterious sounds and sights of the forest. But the manito was always present ~ although unseen ~ no matter how long or how hard the journey through life. This was the ever-lasting bond between all men, the creatures of the forest, and Cautantowit Himself.

DEER ON SLATE
KNIFE ~ BROOKFIELD, MASS.

BIRD ~
NARRAGANSETT BAY.

ABOVE AMULETS, $\frac{3}{4}$ X, FROM WILLIAM FOWLER'S DRAWINGS, MASSACHUSETTS ARCHEOLOGICAL BULLETIN, VOL. 27 No. 3+4 APRIL-JULY 1966 ~ PAGE 44.

There were other manitos ~ enough to boggle the minds of the early Pilgrims and Puritans. Roger Williams counted a total of thirty-eight. They included the Gods of the East, West, North and South, the House God, and Women's God. When Williams took issue with the Narragansetts and their Fire-God, he was told "..... this fire must be a God, or Divine power, that out of a

COPPER THUNDERBIRD, MANCHESTER, N.H.
PEABODY MUSEUM, CAMBRIDGE.

stone will arise in a sparke and when a poore naked *Indian* is ready to starve with cold in the House, and especially in the Woods, often saves his life, doth dresse all our Food for us, and if it be angry will burne the House about us, yea if a spark fall into the drie wood, burns up the Country, (though this burning of the Wood to them they count a Benefit both for destroying of vermin, and keeping downe the Weeds and thickets.)"

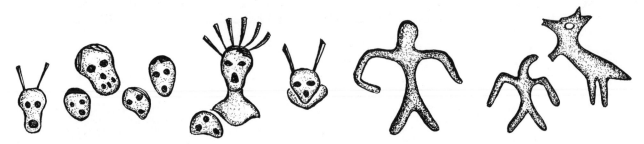

REPRESENTATIVE INDIAN SCULPTURES IN VERMONT ROCK. THE CHIEF AND HIS TRIBE TO THE LEFT MAY TELL OF A NOTABLE EXPLOIT ~ ON TWO ROCKS AT THE FOOT OF BELLOWS FALLS, VERMONT. FIGURES ON THE RIGHT SHOW TWO POSSIBLE THUNDERBIRDS AND AN ANIMAL ~ PERHAPS A MANITO ~ LOCATED AT BRATTLEBORO NEAR THE JUNCTION OF THE WANTASTIQUET AND THE CONNECTICUT RIVER. THE SCULPTURES ARE SOMETIMES UNDERWATER.

Natural wonders were also among the lesser gods. There was the Sun~God and the Moon~God. The Thunder and Lightning God belonged to the heavens where only a bird could fly, and was represented as such since the Late Archaic days. White settlers dubbed it the "Thunderbird."

Every success or calamity was a result of favor or anger from one of the manitos. This lesser god would be pleased with feasting to celebrate a good fortune. A "spirited" dance might appease a show of anger. Amulets ~ representations of these spirits ~ would also keep the wearer safe from misfortune or disease.

SHAMAN ~ also called Powwaw

or Medicine man, was basically a doctor rather than a priest. His prestigious position had little to do with medicinals, but instead an ability to communicate with and to control the world of spirits. Extraordinary dreams and visions were proof of his powers. Because disease was caused by an angry spirit, he was able to use his supernatural powers to intervene on behalf of the patient. Other than driving off these evil spirits, he was not a religious leader of the Algonquin people.

The Ceramic~Woodland shaman was still something of a magician, although he no longer used the tubes of the old Adena culture days. He might mystify the onlookers by thrusting a knife into the empty air, then bringing it back covered with blood. He could make animal spirits talk out

70

of the darkness. The Sun God spoke through the beat of his medicine drum, and the Moon God's voice was the rattle of the tortoise shell.

Before beginning his mystical cure, the shaman required a fee for service. The larger the contribution, the longer and more spectacular the ritual. His dress was that of a bird, beast or some fearful monster. He first called on the gods with his songs and gestures gradually increasing the tempo and loudness of his voice ~ as well as the violence of his motions. Finally he punctuated the whole with wild howls and shouts. The sick patient might occasionally muster a few words of approval, or even join in on the chant. Concluding the treatment, the shaman breathed a few times into the face of the patient before taking his leave.

The shaman was not without assistance. Frequently he called upon animal spirit helpers. His medicine bag contained an image or manito of one or more of these animal spirit assistants, as well as a collection of bark, roots, sticks and sometimes a flute or whistle. As for the curing of such usual illnesses as stomach aches, sprains, sores and the like ~ these were left to the squaw and her herbs.

THE LAST JOURNEY

~ When the women of the family gathered about the sick bed, they blacked their faces with soot or charcoal. But when the ill member left this world for the peace of the southwest, the men also blackened their faces in sorrow. Tears and wailing punctuated the death scene, sometimes extending for months ~ or even a year if the deceased were prominent or of high office. At no time was the dead called by name, and more than once a war began when a dead sachem was named by the leader of a neighboring tribe.

The bereaved were kept very much in mind. Visitors called frequently, saying "Kutchímmoke" ("Be of good cheer"). They expressed their grief by stroking the cheek and head of each member of the family.

A wise and respected man of the tribe conducted the burial rites. While both men and women wept openly, he decorated the body with whatever ornaments the family could afford. He then wrapped the deceased in a protection of mats or furs, taking care to place the body in extreme flexion, the hands before the face. Meanwhile, the shallow grave was dug in a northeast ~ southwest line. The bottom was lined with a cushion of branches and sticks. The body was generally laid to rest on the right side, head to the southwest facing east.

71

Sometimes it was laid on its back with the back of the head facing to the southwest. Weapons, tools and dishes of food were laid alongside, ready for the great journey to Cautantowit. As each shovelful hid the wrapped form from view, the weeping and wailing increased.

On occasion, a mat or dish was laid beside the grave, and some of the remaining clothing hung from a nearby tree. There they remained until they turned to dust, for no man would touch them. To do so might mean that the departed spirit must wander alone, naked and hungry.

NEARLY ALL OF THE WELL-PRESERVED SKELETONS IN NEW ENGLAND ARE NOT OLDER THAN THE BEGINNING OF THE 16TH CENTURY.

Sacrifices were sometimes made to appease the wrath of the god who had filled the dead with sickness or injury. The more notable the dead person, the larger the offering might be. After the death of a son of Canonicus, grand-sachem of the Narragansetts, the grieving father set fire to his wigwam and all it contained.

PENDANTS ~ Protection for the living and dead.

Drawn $\frac{3}{4}$ X

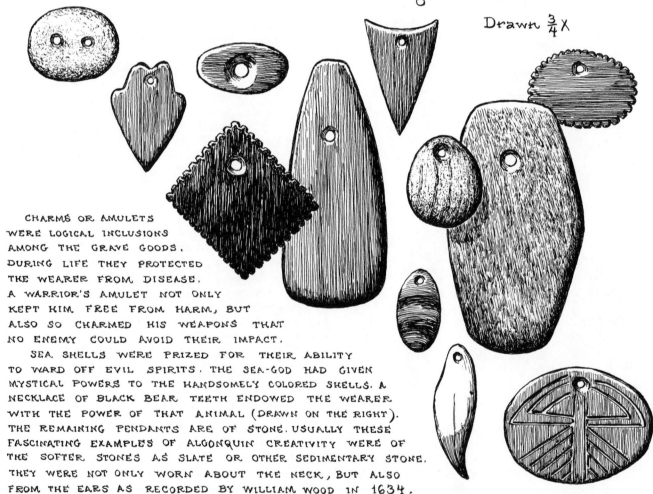

CHARMS OR AMULETS WERE LOGICAL INCLUSIONS AMONG THE GRAVE GOODS. DURING LIFE THEY PROTECTED THE WEARER FROM DISEASE. A WARRIOR'S AMULET NOT ONLY KEPT HIM FREE FROM HARM, BUT ALSO SO CHARMED HIS WEAPONS THAT NO ENEMY COULD AVOID THEIR IMPACT.

SEA SHELLS WERE PRIZED FOR THEIR ABILITY TO WARD OFF EVIL SPIRITS. THE SEA-GOD HAD GIVEN MYSTICAL POWERS TO THE HANDSOMELY COLORED SHELLS. A NECKLACE OF BLACK BEAR TEETH ENDOWED THE WEARER WITH THE POWER OF THAT ANIMAL (DRAWN ON THE RIGHT). THE REMAINING PENDANTS ARE OF STONE. USUALLY THESE FASCINATING EXAMPLES OF ALGONQUIN CREATIVITY WERE OF THE SOFTER STONES AS SLATE OR OTHER SEDIMENTARY STONE. THEY WERE NOT ONLY WORN ABOUT THE NECK, BUT ALSO FROM THE EARS AS RECORDED BY WILLIAM WOOD IN 1634.

72

THE HISTORIC PERIOD ~

The sudden influx of European traders and explorers at the beginning of the seventeenth century marked the beginning of the Historic period. Although their brief visits to the New England shores were occasionally clouded by cheating, skirmishes and ambushes, and kidnapings, the bulk of the Algonquin people were little influenced ~ or even aware ~ of those foreign contacts.

When the Pilgrims gained their Plymouth toehold in 1620, any misgivings between the two races faded from memory. Those high-minded Englishmen brought with them a deep and sincere friendship for the natives that endured for over fifty years.

Well before the Puritan settlement, the Ceramic-Woodland culture had fallen on hard times. Their early creative thrust had been blunted by centuries of bloody warfare. Then the great plague of 1616~1617 riddled much of the remaining Indian population. There were those tribes with scarcely enough living to bury the dead. Old enemies fell on their weakened neighbors. The tribes of New England were well on the trail to self-destruction.

Abnaki ~ New England's northernmost tribe were hunters, not farmers. Untouched by the epidemics, these dread and cruel Tarrantines (as they were called by the tribes to the south) warred on the disease-ridden tribe called the Massachusetts.

Pennacooks ~ Staggered by illness, they were no longer a threat to the easily subjugated Nipmucs.

Massachusetts ~ Reduced from three thousand to five hundred tribesmen by the epidemic, they welcomed protection of the newly arrived Puritans.

Nausets ~ A small Cape Cod tribe, made smaller by the epidemic. They were related to the Wampanoags.

Wampanoags ~ Like the Massachusetts, they were devastated by the illness. They preserved their survivors from their Narragansett enemies by an alliance with the Pilgrims.

Narragansetts ~ Somehow escaping the epidemic, this powerful tribe of four thousand frequently took to the warpath against their neighbors ~ including the fierce Pequots.

Pequots ~ This most warlike and feared tribe originally migrated from the Mahicans of the upper Hudson River in the late sixteenth century. Originally known as the Mohegans (a corruption of Mahican), they soon earned the name of Pequots ~ Algonquin for "destroyer". The Pequots easily crushed and ruled the weaker southern Connecticut River tribes. In 1637, they were defeated by a combined Indian and colonial army. The only survivors had earlier separated from the main body under Chief Uncas. These dissenters called themselves Mohegans as in earlier days.

The **Montauks** of Long Island were in constant conflict with not only the Pequots, but also the Narragansetts and Niantics.

Niantics–No match for the Pequots, the tribe was split in two by the enemy's invasion. The western half fell under the heavy hand of the Pequots, but the eastern half came under the protection of the Narragansetts.

River Indians~ Small tribes, scattered along the lower Connecticut River, were related to the Wappinger tribes of lower New York. They were easily overpowered by the Pequots.

Pocumtucks~ These loosely knit tribes along the Massachusetts portion of the Connecticut River were fair game for the most fierce and aggressive tribes of all, the Mohawks. All Algonquins feared their ruthless invasions ~ and especially their cannibalism.

Nipmucs~ This group of weak tribes were periodically mauled by the Pennacooks, Massachusetts, Wampanoags and the Pequots.

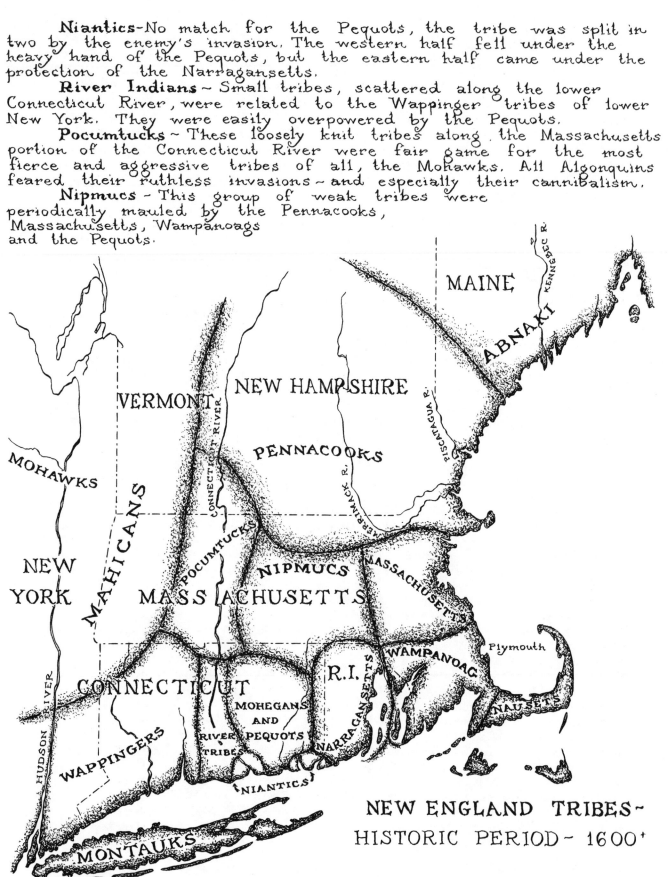

NEW ENGLAND TRIBES ~
HISTORIC PERIOD ~ 1600⁺

74

THE SPOKEN WORD ~

The Algonquin language is very much with us today. Such words as sachem, squaw, papoose, quahoug, hominy, succotash and tomahawk are but a few in our vocabulary. But there were many other single words that confounded English translation. Take "beaver", for example. Each tribe had its own version. To the north, the Abnaki called it "tmakwa" (cuts wood), while the neighboring Malecite and Passamaquoddy named it "kwabit" (ugly teeth) or "Ketaaag-a-naoloss" (rough tailed one). To the south, Roger Williams wrote that the Narragansetts used "Tummock quaûog", "Noosup" and "Sumhup" to represent that single English word "beaver".

In spite of such differences in tribal words and dialects, the sentence structure and some words were like enough for understanding between tribes. Positioning of descriptive adverbs and adjectives was familiar to all the New England natives. The speech might be different but the thought the same.

If all this was confusing to the European newcomers, the compounding of Indian words was a real head-scratcher. By joining the sounds that best expressed each individual word, a new word was created. Sometimes lengthy enough to fill a full sentence, the compound word was actually a description. Place-names were typical. It was a word picture that could be used as a road map by the forest-wise native. "Mattawamkeag" (at the mouth of the bar) was born of such parents as "Madaweik" (mouth of a stream) and "amkeag" (gravel bar or sand beach). According to Cotton Mather, these compound words made up nearly a half of the Algonquin language.

PLACE NAMES of New England ~ representative samples of these picture words.

ACADIA = THE EARTH.
AGAWAM = LOWLAND.
ALAMOOSUC = LITTLE DOG PLACE.
ALGONQUIN = PEOPLE OF THE OTHER SHORE.
ANDROSCOGGIN = FISH-CURING PLACE.
APPALACHIAN = PEOPLE OF THE OTHER SIDE.
APPONAUG = OYSTER OR SHELL-FISH.
AQUIDNECK = THE ISLAND.
AROOSTOOK = SHINING RIVER.
ASCUTNEY = AT THE END OF THE RIVER FORK.
ASSINIPPI = ROCKY WATER.
ASSONET = AT THE ROCK.
CARIBOU = DIGGER.
CASCO = MUDDY.
CHAPPAQUIDDICK = SEPARATED ISLAND.
CHEPACHET = RIVER FORK.
CHICOPEE = RUSHING WATER.
COCHITUATE = SWIFT RIVER.
COHASSET = YOUNG PINE LAND.
CONNECTICUT = AT THE LONG ESTUARY.
CONTOOCOOK = PINY RIVER BANK.
COOS = PINE TREE.
CUMMAQUID = HARBOR.

CUTTYHUNK = THING THAT LIES OUT IN THE SEA.
DAMARISCOTTA = RIVER OF LITTLE FISHES.
HAMMONASSETT = SANDBAR.
HOOSAC = MOUNTAIN ROCK.
HOUSATONIC = OVER THE MOUNTAIN.
IROQUOIS = REAL ADDERS (NO LOVE LOST HERE BY ALGONQUINS!)
KENNEBEC = LONG WATER LAND.
KENNEBUNK = LONG SANDBAR.
LASHAWAY = BETWEEN.
MANHASSET = SHELTERED PLACE.
MANITOOK = GOD'S COUNTRY.
MASHPOAG = BAD WATER.
MASSACHUSETTS = PEOPLE OF THE GREAT HILL COUNTRY.
MASSAPOAG = GREAT WATER.
MATCHUK = BADLANDS.
MERIDEN = PLEASANT VALLEY.
MERRIMAC = RAPIDS.
MINGO = TREACHEROUS (ANOTHER TERM FOR IROQUOIS.)
MINNECHAUG = BERRY-LAND.
MISHAWUM = GREAT NECK.
MISQUAMICUT = WELL WOODED COUNTRY.
MOHAWK = CANNIBALS OR COWARDS.

MONAHEGAN = GRAND ISLAND.
MONOMONACK = LOOKOUT POINT.
MONTAUK = IN THE ISLAND COUNTRY.
MYSTIC = GREAT TIDAL RIVER.
NANTUCKET = FAR OFF AMONG THE WAVES.
NARRAGANSETT = PEOPLE OF THE POINT.
NASHUA = THE LAND BETWEEN.
NATICK = MY HOME.
NAUGATUCK = ONE TREE.
NIANTIC = TIDAL LAND.
NOANK = IT IS A POINT.
NONOTUCK = MIDDLE OF THE RIVER.
OSSIPEE = ROCKY RIVER.
PASCOAG = RIVER FORK.
PASSUMPSIC = FLOWING OVER CLEAR
    SANDY BOTTOM.
PAWTUXET = LITTLE FALLS.
PEMAQUID = LONG POINT.
PEMIGEWASSET = LONG RAPIDS.
PENACOOK = WHERE THE PATH IS
    NARROW.
PENOBSCOT = ROCKY SLOPE.
PEQUOT = THE DESTROYERS.
PISQUATAQUIS = AT THE RIVER FORKS.
PODUNK = PLACE WHERE THE FOOT SINKS.
QUECHEE = QUICK, WHIRLING FALLS.
QUIDNECK = BEYOND THE HILL.
QUINEBAUG = LONG POND.
QUINNIPIAC = LONG WATER LAND.
    (NAME FOR NEW HAVEN.)
QUONSET = BOUNDARY.
SACO = OUTFLOWING.
SAGADAHOC = SWIFT WATER FLOWING
    NEAR THE SEA.

SAKONNET = PLACE OF BLACK GEESE.
SARANAC = RIVER OF SUMAC TREES.
SASCO = MARSH.
SAUGATUCK = TIDAL RIVER OUTLET.
SAUGUS = SWAMP.
SAWQUID = PLEASANT POINT.
SCANTIC = WHERE THE RIVER BRANCHES.
SCITUATE = COLD BROOK.
SEBAGO = BIG LAKE.
SEEKONK = WILD GOOSE.
SHAWOMET = A SPRING, OR PLACE TO
    WHICH BOATS GO.
SHETUCKET = LAND BETWEEN RIVERS.
SKOWHEGAN = A PLACE FOR WAITING AND
    WATCHING.
SQUAM = PLEASANT WATER PLACE.
SUNAPEE = ROCKY POND.
SUNCOOK = ROCKY POINT.
TACONIC = WILDERNESS.
TITICUT = AT THE GREAT RIVER.
TUCKERNUCK = LOAF OF BREAD.
UMBAGOG = CLEAR LAKE.
WEATAUG = AT THE VILLAGE.
WEEKAPAUG = AT THE END OF THE POND.
WEEPOWAUG = NARROW CROSSING.
WEYBOSSETT = AT THE CROSSING PLACE.
WINNIPESAUKEE = LAKELAND.
WINNISQUAM = SALMON-FISHING WATERS.
WINOOSKI = WILD ONIONS.
WISCASSET = AT THE HIDDEN OUTLET.
WOONSOCKET = A PLACE OF DEEP DESCENT.
WORONOCO = WINDING ABOUT.
YANKEE = INDIAN PRONUNCIATION OF
    "ENGLISH" ("YENGUESE").

PERSONAL NAMES ~ There were no family

names ~ only individual. An infant was usually named by a prominent tribesman, matron or grandmother. Boys were honored with the name of a deceased Indian, an object or a phenomenon of the heavens. "Little Thunderer," "Returning Cloud," or "A Bird In Continued Flight In The Higher Air" were common. If named after a living warrior, the name was changed slightly, as "Great Eagle" from "White Eagle."

Girls were named from the surface of the earth, the vegetable kingdom or the waters. "The Woman Of The Passing Stream," "The Woman Of The Green Valley" or "The Woman Of The Rock" were frequently used. However, these were secret and sacred names and not to be revealed. Instead, the mother gave them common nicknames such as "Little Fox," "Bad Boy," "Bird," and such terms of endearment. Therefore, the child was always known by these secondary names.

MARK OF KING PHILIP.

MARK OF MIANTONOMO.

MARK OF THE SQUAW
SACHEM AWASHONKS.

UNCAS.

CANONICUS.

WABAN.

OWENECO.

ATTAWANHOOD.

APPEARANCE ~

For nine thousand years, the New England Indian could only tell his story through the artifacts he had fashioned and left behind. His ability to survive and live in harmony with the forests and waters of the northeast never included a means of recording his history. When a trickle of sixteenth century European traders wrote of their observations, the Algonquin people entered into the Historic era. Although occasionally colored by different standards and values, the accounts were reasonably accurate.

These and later eyewitnesses were quick to admire the physical appearance of the natives. They were tall, straight, muscular and well proportioned. Obesity and deformities were rare indeed. Their cheekbones were high and prominent - the eyes widely separated. William Wood in 1634 added "·····high foreheaded, black ey'd, out-nosed, out-breasted, small wasted, lanke bellied, well thighed, flat kneed, handsome growne leggs, and small feete·····."

The skin was a light tawny or bronzed color, and remarkably smooth and clear. Painting of the face was common with both men and women. Red was the preferred color. It was also liberally spread over the body - and indeed, many of their possessions. The bulk of this paint was brought from the iron outcrops near Katahdin and elsewhere in central Maine. This love of staining the body red was the reason the early explorers called them "red men." Bear grease, with or without coloring, protected the skin from insects and chill. At times, the body was smoked with burning sage, sweetgrass or such aromatic plants.

Men rarely used other decorative paints unless on the warpath. Every warrior painted himself as he wished - always with the hope of frightening his enemies. He was an expert with background colors, figures of birds and animals, and particularly the clan symbols across his chest. Various colors, especially black, yellow and vermilion, were kept in small individual bags. There were also bags of fat, used to mix the dry pigments into a paste. These were contained in a larger bag and carried by both men and women.

Tattooing was popular. Symbols of the bear, wolf and tortoise were among the permanent decorations on clan members. The skin was pierced with a sharp stone or bone sliver and a black dye worked into the deeper layers. Cheeks were a usual target. Some went a step further by burning designs into the skin with a hot tool, sometimes searing a length along the lateral arms.

HAIR was straight, black and glossy - and no lack of it. Baldness was a rarity. No boy could wear his hair long until he reached maturity at the age of sixteen. Then, like his elders, he would pamper his hanks more than the womenfolk. It was dressed daily with bear fat to give it a sheen, and frequently soot was added to deepen the natural black color.

Hair styles were limited only by the wearer's imagination. The most popular was the cockscomb~a strip of hair running down the center of the head (1.) The hairdo was kept short and stiff with paints and grease~the sides of the scalp were shaved or plucked. Philip's Wampanoag warriors preferred this style. Often artificial roaches of deer bristles, dyed to a brilliant red, were tied to the head to heighten the effect.

    Others wore the hair to the shoulders, in which case it might be braided (2.) or left trailing down the back of the head like a scalp lock (3.). Bits of shells, stones, metal and the like were often tied into the hair for decoration. Some tied the crown hair into a top knot (4.) or let it dangle down, much like a horse's tail. Others shaved their head on one side and let the hair grow long on the other (5.) And there were those who shaved all but a small tuft, the scalp lock, at the back of the head (6.) It was an invitation for the enemy to grab the hairy handle as a trophy - if he dared. As William Wood noted in his "New England's Prospect," "·····other cuts they have as their fancie befools them, which would torture the wits of a curious Barber to imitate."

ARTIFICIAL ROACH OF DEER HAIR, DYED RED.

    The warrior, for all his attention to his head of hair, had only dis- tain for hair elsewhere. Although facial and body hair was scant by nature, he made it more so by plucking any offending shafts.

HEADDRESSES ~ Hats were unknown, but
headbands of embroidered skin were worn by both men and women. The skin of the black hawk was highly prized. White feathered bird skins, a fox tail or a rattlesnake skin were a reasonable second best. Other bands were dyed black. There were bangles and fancy tails hang- ing down, and as the Historic period contin- ued, wampum sewn to the band itself was

QUAHAUG ~
NATURE'S READY-MADE TWEEZERS.

the ultimate in finery.

Feathers, secured to the band, were usually from the eagle, hawk or turkey. They were usually arranged in an upright position that resembled a fan, or sometimes hung down from behind. There is evidence that only the most outstanding warriors wore the scarce eagle tail feathers - each representing an enemy life taken in battle. As for the showy war bonnets of the plains Indians - they had no place in the dress of the Algonquin New Englander.

BREECH CLOUTS

~ Until the age of ten or twelve, boys ran about in the warm weather as naked as a jay bird. Both men and women wore this covering of doe or seal skin. A yard and a half long, it was suspended from a belt or girdle with flaps hanging down in front and back. It was frequently the only garment worn by the men around camp.

MANTLES

or shoulder capes were fastened over the left shoulder and hung under the right arm to allow for full motion. On the trail, the mantle was secured at the waist with a belt. This belt was sometimes hollow to carry a supply of parched corn for the journey.

There were mantles for warm weather, woven from hemp or grass. Extending down to the thighs, they were worn to discourage mosquitoes. A more elegant variety was of iridescent turkey feathers, interwoven into a network of twine. Each of the small feathers overlapped its neighbor as on the back of the original owner. Elderly tribal men specialized in this tedious job, and women sometimes fashioned feathered mantles for their children. Deerskin, dressed without hair, was usually worn by the warrior. A handsome mantle was also made from moose hide, cured without hair to a fine and uniform milk white surface. Designs along the border were in colors of red, yellow and blue.

Mantles for cold weather were logically dressed with the fur intact. The furred side was worn next to the body. Bear, moose, deer, wolf, beaver, otter, fox, raccoon, and squirrel pelts were used. But raccoon was the favorite, for when the skins were sewn together, the trailing tails gave a striking appearance. As for the deer mantle, a perfect tail or "flag" was greatly admired. One bear, moose or deer hide was large enough for a single mantle. The free right arm was covered with the whole skin of the bobcat.

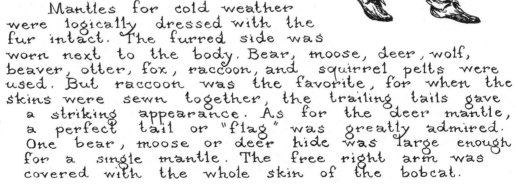

TWILLED WOVEN
MANTLE OF BAST.

79

Occasionally, otter and beaver skins also gave warmth with this temporary sleeve.

BELTS or girdles ~

QUILL WORK ON LEATHER BELT. CONJECTURAL.

This multi-purpose wrap-around secured the mantle when traveling, supported the breech clout and leggings, and carried pouches filled with fire making materials, pipe and tobacco. It was crafted of snakeskin or leather (which was sometimes fringed as was Samoset's). Later, it was covered with purple and white wampum beads in symbolic figures. It became not only a sign of wealth but was also given to seal a promise or treaty.

LEGGINGS ~

These leg tubes of deerskin were worn by men. (Women dressed in a lower and shorter style.) One of the most practical articles of clothing, they gave protection from the brush and brambles along the trail, gave warmth and served as a ceremonial dress as well. An oblong of hide was perforated down the two longest sides with a series of awl punch holes, then sewn with sinew to form a cylinder. One for each leg, each was suspended from the belt by lateral thongs, while the lower legging was tied under the foot. Each legging was decorated down it's length and sometimes fringed.

SIDE DECORATIONS.

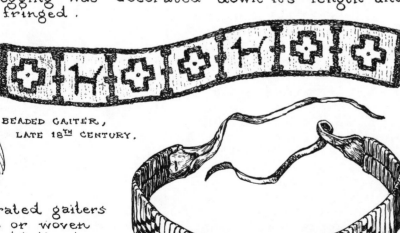

BEADED GAITER, LATE 18TH CENTURY.

Decorated gaiters of hide or woven fiber held the legging snug below the knee.

QUILL DECORATED GAITER, 18TH CENTURY DESIGN.

80

MOCCASINS ~

Here was a real economy of materials, for nine moccasins could be cut from one large buckskin. Moosehide was sturdier and usually preferred. Each moccasin was made from a single piece of hide, with only the sole added. For travel on the woodland carpets of New England, this sole was soft as a stocking. (Plains tribes used a stiff sole similar to that of a slipper to combat the abrasive effects of sharp stones.) In foul weather, the flaps were raised to give added protection. According to available eighteenth century specimens, many moccasins were tied about the ankle for a snug fit. Revere's engraving of King Philip and the oil portrait of Chief Ninigret (circa 1647) at the Rhode Island School of Design show these thong ties.

UNDERSIDE OF MOCCASIN, WITH SOFT LEATHER SOLE STITCHED IN PLACE. EACH MOCCASIN COULD BE WORN ON EITHER FOOT TO EQUALIZE WEAR.

HOLES ABOVE HEEL LIKELY HELD A THONG TIE FOR A BETTER FIT.

SOFT, SMOKE-TANNED BUCKSKIN GAVE MINIMAL PUCKERING WHEN SEWN AT THE TOP SEAM.

QUILL, HEMP, BEAD AND CLOTH-SURFACED FLAPS DECORATE A NORTHAMPTON MASS^{TTS} HISTORICAL SOCIETY MOCCASIN, LATE 18TH CENTURY.

The top seam was covered with a strip of deerskin, decorated with dyed porcupine quills or moose hair. Later, seed beads were added. Both side flaps were also covered with a piece of ornamented hide. Many were faced with trade cloth after the arrival of the colonists. When the dress moccasins were worn out, these handsome and valued designs were transferred to new moccasins. Geometric designs were earlier than the floral work of later pieces. As for everyday work moccasins, there was probably little or no decoration.

POUCHES AND PIPES ~

Many pipes of the Historic period were of wood with carved animals or human faces. Some were massive with a bowl four inches tall and a stem of two feet! Others were of stone, but most were of colonial metal.

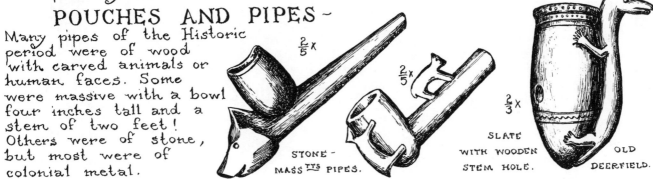

$\frac{2}{5}$ x

STONE-MASS^{TTS} PIPES.

$\frac{2}{5}$ x

SLATE WITH WOODEN STEM HOLE.

$\frac{2}{3}$ x

OLD DEERFIELD.

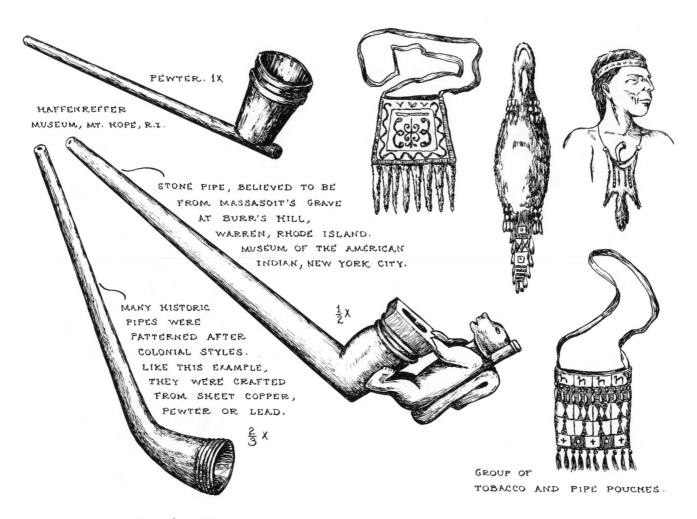

PEWTER. 1X

HAFFENREFFER
MUSEUM, MT. HOPE, R.I.

STONE PIPE, BELIEVED TO BE
FROM MASSASOIT'S GRAVE
AT BURR'S HILL,
WARREN, RHODE ISLAND.
MUSEUM OF THE AMERICAN
INDIAN, NEW YORK CITY.

MANY HISTORIC
PIPES WERE
PATTERNED AFTER
COLONIAL STYLES.
LIKE THIS EXAMPLE,
THEY WERE CRAFTED
FROM SHEET COPPER,
PEWTER OR LEAD.

$\frac{1}{2}$ X

$\frac{2}{3}$ X

GROUP OF
TOBACCO AND PIPE POUCHES.

WOMEN'S WEAR ~ AND TEAR ~

The appearance of the Algonquin women
fell short of the glowing accounts given their
men. Frequently they were described as short and
clumsy and with features less than delicate or
pretty. Repeated pregnancies and a life of hard
labor may well have aged them before their time.
But the girls and young women, not yet bent by
their burdens, were likely every bit as attractive
as their colonial counterparts.

HAIR ~ was glossy black. Dyes were rarely used,
for gray hair was a rarity. Occasionally, however,
vermillion and bear fat were used to spark up
a part of the hair. Long hair was admired, and
indeed it often hung down to the hips. Sometimes it
was gathered into a bunch down the back ~ much like
a beaver tail ~ or braided. Occasionally the hair over
the forehead was trimmed into bangs.

$\frac{2}{3}$ X

ANTLER COMB,
VINALHAVEN, MASSACHUSETTS.
PEABODY MUSEUM, CAMBRIDGE, MASSACHUSETTS.

METAL COMB FROM PRINCESS
NINIGRET'S GRAVE,
CHARLESTOWN, RHODE ISLAND.
R.I. HISTORICAL SOCIETY.

SKIN

SKIN ~ was kept smooth with fish oil and eagle fat. As with the men, red pigment was mixed to give a reddish coloration. In addition, bright red was applied to the forehead, temples and cheeks. Young women favored a black pigment around the eyes and on the forehead. The body also received its share of decorative paints.

SKIRT

SKIRT - Well before the arrival of the colonists, women wore only the breech clout in warm weather or about the wigwam. By the time the Historic period opened, all women wore a knee length skirt. Indeed, no woman would consider being seen without her skirt ~ and that was all, unless chill weather or ceremonial dress dictated otherwise. The skirts were simple, requiring only a rectangular piece of deerskin. It must be wide enough to wrap around the waist. The slightly overlapping edges fell over the right thigh. A belt held the Algonquin slit skirt, as it was known to the settlers, in proper position.

ALGONQUIN SLIT SKIRT WITH SHORT LEGGINGS.

MANTLES

MANTLES ~ Longer and fuller than that of the warriors', the squaws' mantle took two deer or bear skins stitched together down their length. This cold weather covering was so long that it sometimes dragged on the ground. Morton observed that they were "....like a great ladies train." Occasionally a shorter mantle, a sort of a jacket, was worn as an upper covering.

WOMAN'S MANTLE.

LEGGINGS

LEGGINGS - The squaws' leggings were quite a different sort. Each skin tube covered only the lower leg, beginning just below the knees. A garter held each in place. Ornamentation was only at the lower border where it ended just below the ankle. As with the men's leggings, they were fastened within the moccasins to keep out the rain or snow.

MOCCASINS

MOCCASINS ~ were similar to the men's footgear.

COLONIAL INFLUENCE ~

As with much of the Algonquin culture, clothing was strongly influenced by the influx of settlers. The warrior could trade his pelts for ten times the value of woven cloth. Although hides absorbed perspiration and were therefore more sanitary than the new

SHEET COPPER OR BRASS BRACELET FROM THE GRAVE OF PRINCESS NINIGRET, CHARLESTOWN, R.I., SHOWING THE EUROPEAN INFLUENCE OVER INDIAN CRAFTS.

R.I. HISTORICAL SOCIETY.

woolen goods, it was no contest. Cloth trade blankets made the mantle obsolete. European shirts, jackets, pants and dresses replaced the traditional wear, although initially the material was patterned after the old skin garments. Erosion of the old Algonquin ways was gaining momentum.

THE MYSTERY OF PHILIP'S "ROYALTIES" ~ BENJAMIN CHURCH'S "HISTORY OF KING PHILIP'S WAR" (NEWPORT, 1772) DISPLAYS THIS QUESTIONABLE ETCHING OF THE WAMPANOAG SACHEM. THE SQUAT AND DOUR FIGURE WAS BORROWED FROM AN UNRELATED PAINTING, AND JIBES NOT AT ALL WITH THE OLD HISTORICAL ACCOUNTS. THE MUSKET WAS FROM A SECOND PAINTING, AND LIKE THE TRADE BLANKET, COLONIAL SHIRT AND TRADITIONAL MOCCASINS, WAS REASONABLY ACCURATE. THE EUROPEAN INFLUENCE WAS HEAVY ON THE NEW ENGLAND INDIAN ~ INCLUDING THEIR REBELLIOUS CHIEFTAIN.

HIS FINE WAMPUM "ROYALTIES" MAY OR MAY NOT BE TRUE REPRESENTATIONS. GIVEN TO THE VICTORIOUS CHURCH AFTER THE DEATH OF PHILIP, THEIR PRESENT WHEREABOUTS REMAINS A MYSTERY. PERHAPS THE DISCOVERY OF THE CENTURY WILL TAKE PLACE IN SOME DUSTY LONG FORGOTTEN NEW ENGLAND ATTIC!

BEADS AND DECORATIONS ~

These, too, fell victim to the vast range of metals and glass that poured in from overseas.

PHILIP. *KING* of Mount Hope.

Before foreign contact, the Indian's hair was decorated with bird skins, animal claws and shell beads. The ear lobes were frequently pierced to receive pendants, feathers, eagle claws and whatever taste dictated. Noses, unlike those of the western Indians, were rarely pierced.

SHELL BEADS ~ Prehistoric craftsmen perforated their shell beads with a very thin stone drill or a wooden drill dipped in wet sand. Turning out disc and tube-shaped beads in this manner was both tedious and slow. The finished product was highly prized; but, as Bradford in his "History of Plymouth Plantation" observed, only "...ye sachems and some speciall persons...wore a little of it for ornaments."

1X

OLD SHELL PREHISTORIC BEADS FROM THE COLUMN OF FULGAR CARICA.

Then, by the 1620's, the making of shell beads became a booming native industry. Dutch traders brought an amount of Long Island Indian beads to Plymouth for trade. Metal awls and nails could drill them in quantity; the Narragansetts (and to some extent, the Pequots) were quick to realize the potential. Entire families and workshops went into production. With a ready supply of quahougs available, coastal Rhode Island and Connecticut became a sort of Indian

84

PERIWINKLES, SMALL COUSINS OF THE RAW MATERIAL THAT BECAME THE LARGE OLD CYLINDRICAL BEADS, COULD BE USED FOR THE NEW AND SMALLER WAMPUM.

1X   THE NEW METAL DRILL POINTS MADE SMALLER PERFORATED CYLINDERS POSSIBLE. THE OUTER SHELL WAS CRUSHED, LEAVING THE CENTER COLUMN. WHITE WAMPUM FROM THIS SOURCE WAS CONSIDERABLY LESS THAN FROM THE QUAHOUG.

BOW DRILL.

IRON WAMPUM DRILL, SQUARE CROSS-SECTION, FORT SHANTOK, CONN.

QUAHOUG.

THE SMALL PURPLE TO BLACK PORTION OF THE QUAHOUG MADE "SUCKAUHOCK" (SÁCKI = BLACK). THE BULK OF THE SHELL WAS WHITE AND GAVE THE "WOMPAM"~ MEANING WHITE).

DISC BLANKS.

CYLINDER BLANKS.

THE SHELLS WERE BROKEN AND ROUGHLY TRIMMED TO SIZE. AFTER PERFORATION WITH THE BOW DRILL'S METAL POINT, THE PIECES WERE STRUNG ON HEMP.

mint. The beads ~ or wampum ~ became the equivalent of the white man's money. Each bead was turned out so well that glass counterfeiting was near impossible.

Down east in Maine, the Abnakis were caught up in the wampum bonanza. They became widely known for their finely woven shell bead ear pendants, collars, gaiters ~ and sashes that were as wide as five or six inches. Throughout New England, men, women and children wore their new wampum in imaginative designs, weaving their wealth into caps, aprons, belts, neck ornaments, bags, wallets, moccasins and every sort of personal wear.

The more important the personage, the more dazzling the display. One of King Philip's belts was nine inches wide. When hung around his neck, it came clear to his ankles. The sachem also owned two other belts ~ one with two flags which hung from his head (likely his headband) and the other with a star on its end that rested on his chest. Revere's engraving shows this clearly. Further, when Philip visited Boston in 1671, his coat, buskins and belt were studded with £20 worth of wampum. This was a kingly fortune, for English merchants were offering ten shillings a fathom for white beads, and double that

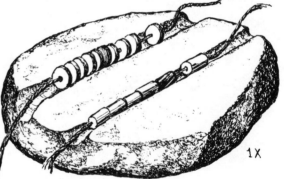

THE STRINGS WERE WORKED IN THE GROOVES OF THE GRINDSTONE UNTIL THE EDGES WERE SMOOTH, ROUND AND UNIFORM.

1X   STRING OF DISC WAMPUM.

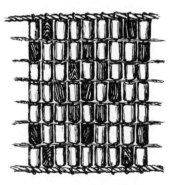

DETAIL 3X   WAMPUM BELT 1X

amount for purple . (When strung, cylindrical wampum averaged five to the inch, or three hundred and sixty for six feet or a fathom.)

GLASS BEADS ~
The bulk of the glass trade beads were turned out at the island of Murano as Venetian glass and the Amsterdam glassworks. It was all imported during the Historic period. There is no archaeological evidence that the Jamestown glassworks produced any sort of bead.

A brief word about their manufacture. A thick pear-shaped bubble was first blown from molten glass. If any colored stripes were to be added, strings of varicolored glass were fused to the surface of the bubble. This hot hollow glob was then pulled out to a long thin tube with a center hole. When cool, beads of various sizes could be filed and broken free. Since most required smooth, rounded edges, the beads were tumbled in a hot iron drum filled with fine sand and ashes or clay. This mixture not only prevented the beads from fusing together, but also smoothed off any sharp edges by abrasion. After cooling and washing, they were ready for the American trade.

CLASSIFICATION
of glass beads is an ongoing task. The Indian Glass Bead Repository at the Fort Stanwix Museum, Rome, New York is presently spearheading the investigation. Peter Pratt, Archaeologist of the museum, has written an excellent comparison guide. His time sequence, along with a few New England discoveries, have been generalized in the following sampler. As local examples are added to the Repository's lists, the reader should have more precise information.

1570 ~ 1625 ~

OVAL ~ $\frac{1}{8}$th INCH IN DIAMETER AND $\frac{3}{8}$ths OR LESS IN LENGTH. MOSTLY WHITE PORCELAIN-LIKE, WITH FEWER BLACK AND SOME STRIPED. SOME HAD FLATTENED ENDS .

OVAL ~ MONOCHROMIC OR MULTISTRIPED.

OVAL ~ MULTISTRIPED OF MANY LARGER SIZES.

1625 ~ 1660 ~ IN ADDITION TO THE ABOVE, SOME LONG TUBULAR BEADS WERE INTRODUCED.

TUBULAR ~ AN EARLY GLASS IMITATION OF SHELL WAMPUM.

TUBULAR ~ MONOCHROMIC RED OR BLUE.

1660 ~ 1677 -

OVAL - FLATTENED ENDS · MONOCHROMIC IN WHITE, BLACK, GREEN OR RED.

TUBULAR - MANY MORE WERE INTRODUCED DURING THIS PERIOD, AVERAGING $\frac{1}{16}$th TO $\frac{3}{16}$ths INCH IN DIAMETER AND $\frac{1}{2}$ INCH IN LENGTH. MONOCHROMIC WHITE AND BLACK TO IMITATE WAMPUM, SOME WITH RED AND WHITE STRIPES. OCCASIONALLY ALL RED OR YELLOW.

TUBULAR ~ LIKE SMALLER TUBULARS.

OVALS ~ SMALL WITH FLATTENED ENDS. PREDOMINATELY WHITE OR BLUE. KNOWN AS SEED OR EMBROIDERY BEADS.

The earliest oval trade beads with flattened ends were gradually reduced in size until the tiny seed beads flooded the market. Perhaps the larger varieties added too much weight when sewn to clothing. They came too late for most of the Algonquin people. King Philip's War was past history by 1676 ~ the year that the rebellious Wampanoag sachem was killed. Leaderless, most of the New England tribesmen still surviving had fled to Canada and New York state.

The conclusion is obvious. Any article of New England clothing with these small beads may well be an imposter. Some of our local collections may have relics masquerading as New Englanders, when actually they were a product of western Indian beadwork so popular in the nineteenth century. King Philip's "royalties" presents yet another mystery. This fine seed bead belt, supposedly part of his finery, may not have seen the light of day until after his death.

"KING PHILIP'S BELT"
RHODE ISLAND HISTORICAL SOCIETY.

METAL BEADS ~ Long, copper~sheathed beads were nothing
new. Much earlier, the Adena people imported the scarce copper tubes, pounded from Lake Superior nuggets. By the historic period, sheet copper and brass were in great plenty. Brerton, observing the Indians in Massachusetts in 1602, said "....none of but have chaines, ear-rings, or collars of this metal [copper and brass].... Their chaines are many hollow pieces cemented together, each piece of the bigness of one of our reeds, a finger in length, ten or twelve of them together on a string, which they wear about their necks ① : their collars they wear about their bodies like bandoliers a handful broad, all hollow pieces, like the other, but somewhat shorter, four hundred pieces in a collar, very fine and evenly set together."②

1 X

①

HISTORIC LONG
BEADS OF THIN TRADE COPPER
POUNDED ABOUT A WOODEN FORM
THAT WAS THEN REMOVED, OR LEFT ABOUT AN
ELDER WOOD BASE WITH ITS PITH REMOVED.

②
METHOD OF
STRINGING SHORT SHEET
COPPER BEADS (WILLOUGHBY).

1 X

MINIATURE CYLINDRICAL
METAL BEADS, PERHAPS
FORMED AROUND A
WIRE.

A copper necklace, given to Massasoit by the Pilgrims, was to be used by any of the messengers sent by the sachem to the Plymouth Colony.

QUILL WORK ~

With the availability of fancy glass and sheet metal beads, the time-honored ~ and very tedious ~ quill work decoration largely fell by the wayside. Certainly the porcupine population had no objection to this change of fashion, although each had some forty thousand quills to offer. Warm weather was not the time for plucking, for then the hollow shafts were filled with liquid that could ooze out and spoil the quill work.

QUILLS ~ FINE TO COURSE.

Quills averaged about two and a half inches in length and one sixteenth of an inch in diameter. Fine quills for more delicate designs came from behind the head. After washing and dyeing with plant colorings, the squaw softened each in her mouth or in water just before sewing. The shaft was flattened between the teeth or fingernails, and the dark brown tips were bitten off at that time. On buckskin, the quills were bent and sewn on in the following ways, with the thread or sinew entirely covered.

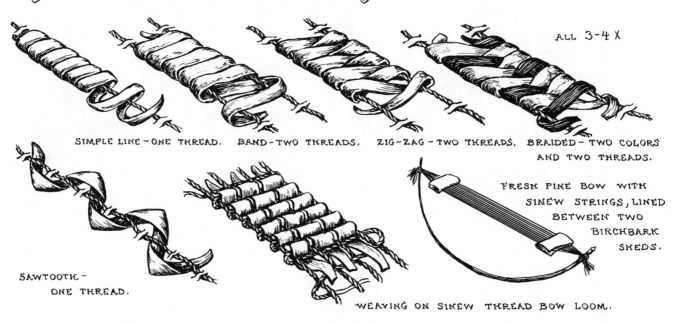

ALL 3-4 X

SIMPLE LINE ~ ONE THREAD.   BAND ~ TWO THREADS.   ZIG~ZAG ~ TWO THREADS.   BRAIDED ~ TWO COLORS AND TWO THREADS.

SAWTOOTH ~ ONE THREAD.

FRESH PINE BOW WITH SINEW STRINGS, LINED BETWEEN TWO BIRCHBARK SHEDS.

WEAVING ON SINEW THREAD BOW LOOM.

For bark designs, the wet quill was threaded through awl holes, then was bent up against the inside surface, much like a staple.

MOOSEHAIR DECORATION ~

This fine embroidery material came from the cheeks, "bell," mane and rump of the moose. Each hair averaged from four to five inches, was white for three-quarters of its length and black at the remaining tip. As with the quillwork, the hairs were washed and dyed, then moistened in water or in the mouth just prior to use. The technique also fell victim to trade bead decoration.

LINE-WORK WAS THE MOST POPULAR. 3 OR 4 STRANDS WERE SEWN ONTO THE LEATHER WITH A DIAGONAL STITCH. BEFORE PULLING THE STITCH TIGHT, THE HAIRS WERE GIVEN A SLIGHT TWIST THAT GAVE A BEAD-LIKE EFFECT.

2-3 X

ZIG-ZAG LINE-WORK. 3 OR 4 HAIRS WERE SEWN BETWEEN 2 PARALLEL LINES OF SINEW THREADS.

AND MORE DECORATIONS ~

"Moons" were shell discs worn as neck ornaments by the historic Algonquin warrior.

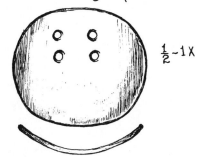

²⁄₃ X

½ ~1 X

1 X

THE WHELK SHELL WAS BROKEN INTO ROUGH DISCS, THEN GROUND THIN AND SMOOTH. ONE OR TWO PAIRS OF HOLES WERE DRILLED FOR THE NECKLACE THONG.

CAST BUTTONS ~

Buttons, small ornaments, pipes and musket balls were cast by the Indian from home made molds cut from slate and soapstone. Pewter and lead had low melting points, and could be handily cast by campfire heat. Brass was also cast but less easily. The molten metal was poured onto the open faced design or down a channel between two molds as with the bullet mold. When cool, the metal was trimmed, then smoothed by grinding.

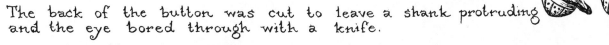

²⁄₃ X

1 X

HALF OF MUSKET BALL MOLD ~ R.I. HISTORICAL SOCIETY.

THREE MOLDS FROM PEABODY MUSEUM, CAMBRIDGE.

The back of the button was cut to leave a shank protruding and the eye bored through with a knife.

FANCY SILVER

from Europe was sometimes presented to the nobility of a tribe. There is no evidence that Indian smiths worked on this metal during the Historic period.

1 X

SILVER BROOCHES FROM THE GRAVE OF A WOMAN THOUGHT TO BE THE DAUGHTER OF CHIEF NINIGRET OF NIANTICS. PEABODY MUSEUM, CAMBRIDGE.

LARGE SILVER PIN. OLD COLONY HISTORICAL SOCIETY, TAUNTON, MASS^TTS.

¾ X

89

BRASS RINGS.

PEWTER BUTTON ~
TYPICAL OF LATE 17TH CENTURY.

BRASS CUFFLINKS.

½ BRASS BELL.

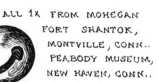

LABOR ~ SAVERS ~ The Historic period

was to the squaw's liking. She
was probably as pleased with
her new work tools as with
her imported jewelry.

BRASS NETTING NEEDLE.
⅔ X

BRASS BLADE FROM A
SAILMAKER'S AWL, FT. SHANTOK.
BOTH ~ PEABODY MUSEUM, NEW HAVEN.

⅔ X

GRUBBING HOE ~
1600-1650, FORT SHANTOK.

And there were trade
goods for her hearth. Fine brass
and copper, as well as cast-iron pots
made her clay pots a second best.

GRUBBING HOE 1650-1700,
FORT SHANTOK. BOTH
HOES DISPLAYED AT THE
PEABODY MUSEUM, NEW HAVEN.

1X

1X

MINIATURE POTS,
1600-1650 A.D.
PRINCESS NINI-
GRET'S GRAVE,
CHARLESTON,
RHODE ISLAND.

R.I. HISTORICAL
SOCIETY, PROVIDENCE,
RHODE ISLAND.

1X

MILES STANDISH'S POT, TYPICAL OF CAST-IRON
POTS ~ FROM STEREOPTICON VIEW 481, KILBURN BROS.,
LITTLETON, N.H.

¼ X ±

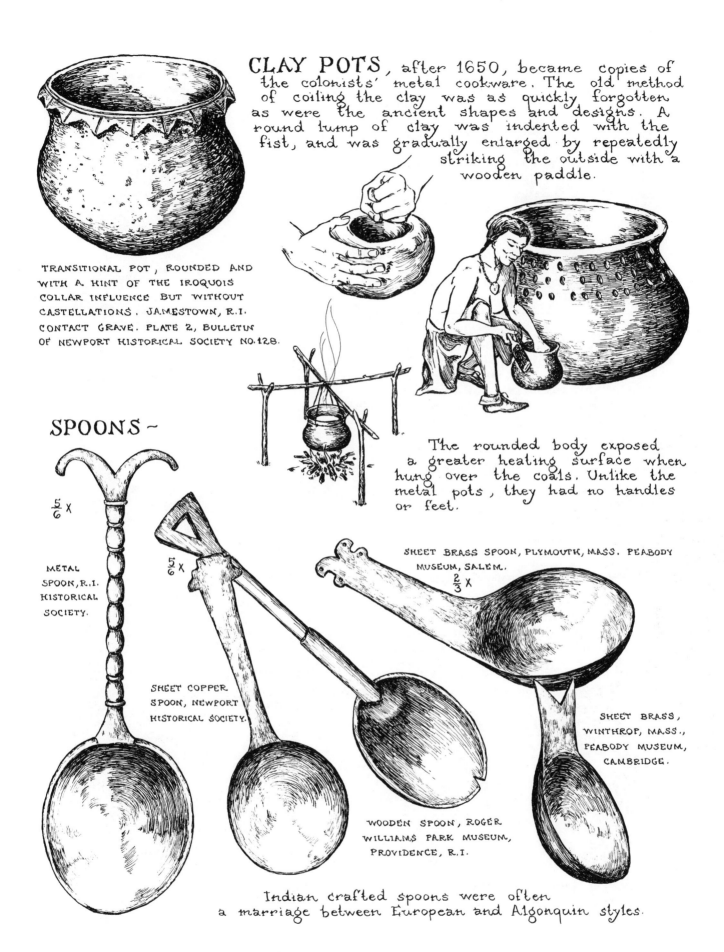

CLAY POTS, after 1650, became copies of the colonists' metal cookware. The old method of coiling the clay was as quickly forgotten as were the ancient shapes and designs. A round lump of clay was indented with the fist, and was gradually enlarged by repeatedly striking the outside with a wooden paddle.

TRANSITIONAL POT, ROUNDED AND WITH A HINT OF THE IROQUOIS COLLAR INFLUENCE BUT WITHOUT CASTELLATIONS. JAMESTOWN, R.I. CONTACT GRAVE. PLATE 2, BULLETIN OF NEWPORT HISTORICAL SOCIETY NO.128.

The rounded body exposed a greater heating surface when hung over the coals. Unlike the metal pots, they had no handles or feet.

SPOONS ~

$\frac{5}{6}$ X

METAL SPOON, R.I. HISTORICAL SOCIETY.

$\frac{5}{6}$ X

SHEET COPPER SPOON, NEWPORT HISTORICAL SOCIETY.

SHEET BRASS SPOON, PLYMOUTH, MASS. PEABODY MUSEUM, SALEM.

$\frac{2}{3}$ X

WOODEN SPOON, ROGER WILLIAMS PARK MUSEUM, PROVIDENCE, R.I.

SHEET BRASS, WINTHROP, MASS., PEABODY MUSEUM, CAMBRIDGE.

Indian crafted spoons were often a marriage between European and Algonquin styles.

CUPS AND BOWLS ~

These soapstone objects tell their own story ~ and the message is disturbing. No hint of the Algonquin heritage here ~ only crude copies of the intruders' possessions. The contact period seemed one of erosion ~ and the Indian seemed eager for changes.

1 X

SOAPSTONE CUP. ROGER WILLIAMS PARK MUSEUM, PROVIDENCE, R.I.

⅗ X

SOAPSTONE GOBLET, HAFFENREFFER MUSEUM, MT. HOPE, RHODE ISLAND.

THE CROOKED KNIFE ~ On the other hand ~ good English steel, salvaged from an old file or even a tired musket barrel, gave new life to the crafting of woodenware. Shunning traditional colonial tools, the Indian fashioned a combination draw knife and gouge. With it, he continued a tradition of bowls and ladles that were every inch a part of his culture.

½ X

½ X

AN OLD FILE WAS GROUND TO LESS THAN $\frac{1}{8}$TH INCH IN THICKNESS, $\frac{5}{8}$THS OF AN INCH WIDE, AND WITH A BLADE OF 4 OR 5 INCHES IN LENGTH. THE UPPER SIDE OF THE BLADE WAS BEVELED DOWN ITS LENGTH, GIVING A CHISEL EDGE.

A BRANCH OF A FORKED STICK WAS REMOVED FOR THE HANDLE.

KNIFE TURNED OVER, SHOWING CURVE AT THE TIP OF THE BLADE. THE TANG AND ITS BENT END WAS INSERTED INTO THE HANDLE AND LASHED IN PLACE.

SOME CROOKED KNIVES HAD A SHARP TANG, WHICH WAS THEN DRIVEN INTO A DRILLED HOLE IN THE HANDLE.

THE KNIFE WAS GRASPED, FINGERS UP, WITH THE THUMB STEADIED AGAINST THE ANGLED END OF THE HANDLE. THIS WAS NO WHITTLING KNIFE.

Since archaic days, liquids were held in wooden containers. The Historic Indian gladly substituted colonial steel for the laborious business of charring and scraping with stone knives, scrapers and adz blades. The burls of such hardwoods as maple, elm, pepperage and cherry swirled the wood grain in a manner not likely to split. These were handsomely carved pieces with stylized effigies for handles. Some had drilled eyes that might hold a thong for hanging.

RATHER, THE CROOKED KNIFE WAS A ONE-HANDED DRAW KNIFE THAT CUT BY PULLING TOWARD THE BODY.

Generally the container had considerable depth with a

92

handle, quite perpendicular to its rim. Drinking cups ~ a direct ancestor of the settler's noggin ~ often had a thong and toggle that could be tucked under the belt.

SIMPLE NOGGIN, HANGING FROM BELT BY TOGGLE.

3/5 X

WAMPANOAG LADLE WITH CARVED BIRD'S HEAD, COLLECTED 1681. HEYE MUSEUM, NEW YORK, N.Y.

1/4 X

1/3 X

NIPMUC DRINKING CUP ~ WILLOUGHBY'S "ANTIQUITIES OF THE NEW ENGLAND INDIANS", P.259.

MAHICAN WOODEN LADLE OR PADDLE. NEW YORK STATE MUSEUM, ALBANY, N.Y.

2/7 X
PEABODY MUSEUM, CAMBRIDGE.

2/7 X

WOODEN BOWL FROM THE GRAVE OF NARRAGANSETT CHIEF MIANANOMO.

SLATER MUSEUM, NORWICH, CONN.

WAMPANOAG ELM BOWL, FORMERLY THOUGHT TO BE FROM THE WIGWAM OF KING PHILIP WHEN SLAIN IN 1676.

GAMES
~ No one, including the bulk of New England's colonists who held to the Puritan work ethic, ever accused the Algonquin warrior, of a liking for hard labor. But when it came to meeting a chancy or an un-certain situation, or when daring, strength, intuition and cunning were needed, the Indian was up to the challenge. His survival in a hostile wilderness depended upon such responses. From the Archaic days, he had sharpened his wits with games of skill or chance.

2/7 X

NIANTIC WOODEN BOWL, PEABODY MUSEUM, NEW HAVEN, CONN.

3/4 X

DICE COUNTERS, CHIPPED FLAT AND SQUARE, WERE COLORED ON ONE SURFACE. WAGERS WERE MADE ON WHICH SURFACE WOULD BE VISABLE WHEN THROWN.

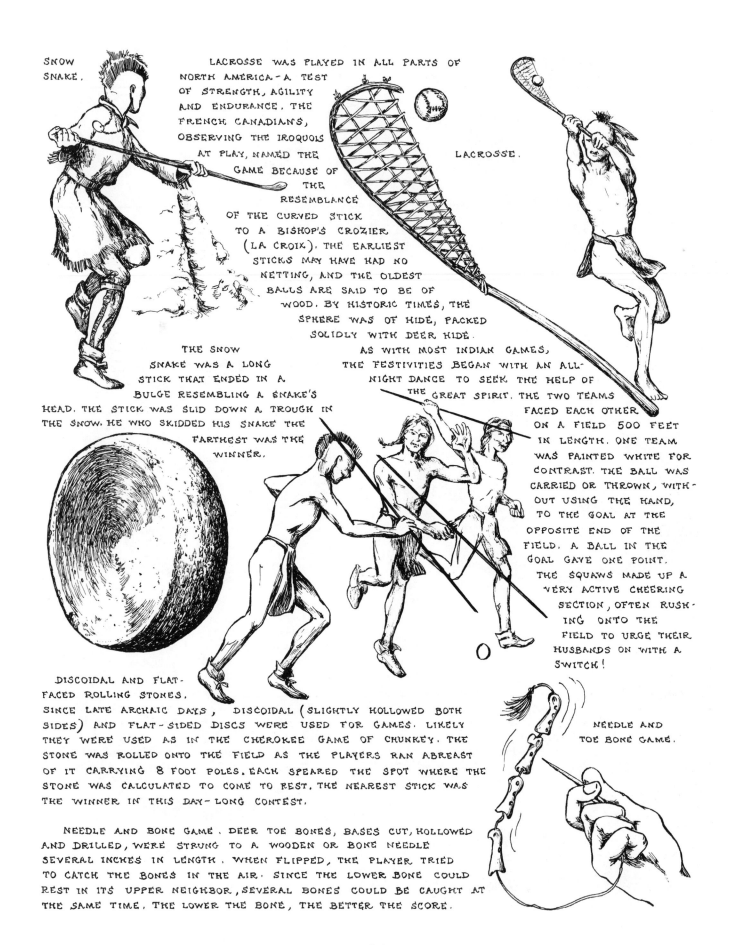

SNOW SNAKE.

LACROSSE WAS PLAYED IN ALL PARTS OF NORTH AMERICA - A TEST OF STRENGTH, AGILITY AND ENDURANCE. THE FRENCH CANADIANS, OBSERVING THE IROQUOIS AT PLAY, NAMED THE GAME BECAUSE OF THE RESEMBLANCE OF THE CURVED STICK TO A BISHOP'S CROZIER (LA CROIX). THE EARLIEST STICKS MAY HAVE HAD NO NETTING, AND THE OLDEST BALLS ARE SAID TO BE OF WOOD. BY HISTORIC TIMES, THE SPHERE WAS OF HIDE, PACKED SOLIDLY WITH DEER HIDE.

LACROSSE.

THE SNOW SNAKE WAS A LONG STICK THAT ENDED IN A BULGE RESEMBLING A SNAKE'S HEAD. THE STICK WAS SLID DOWN A TROUGH IN THE SNOW. HE WHO SKIDDED HIS SNAKE THE FARTHEST WAS THE WINNER.

AS WITH MOST INDIAN GAMES, THE FESTIVITIES BEGAN WITH AN ALL-NIGHT DANCE TO SEEK THE HELP OF THE GREAT SPIRIT. THE TWO TEAMS FACED EACH OTHER ON A FIELD 500 FEET IN LENGTH. ONE TEAM WAS PAINTED WHITE FOR CONTRAST. THE BALL WAS CARRIED OR THROWN, WITHOUT USING THE HAND, TO THE GOAL AT THE OPPOSITE END OF THE FIELD. A BALL IN THE GOAL GAVE ONE POINT. THE SQUAWS MADE UP A VERY ACTIVE CHEERING SECTION, OFTEN RUSHING ONTO THE FIELD TO URGE THEIR HUSBANDS ON WITH A SWITCH!

DISCOIDAL AND FLAT-FACED ROLLING STONES.
SINCE LATE ARCHAIC DAYS, DISCOIDAL (SLIGHTLY HOLLOWED BOTH SIDES) AND FLAT-SIDED DISCS WERE USED FOR GAMES. LIKELY THEY WERE USED AS IN THE CHEROKEE GAME OF CHUNKEY. THE STONE WAS ROLLED ONTO THE FIELD AS THE PLAYERS RAN ABREAST OF IT CARRYING 8 FOOT POLES. EACH SPEARED THE SPOT WHERE THE STONE WAS CALCULATED TO COME TO REST. THE NEAREST STICK WAS THE WINNER IN THIS DAY-LONG CONTEST.

NEEDLE AND TOE BONE GAME.

NEEDLE AND BONE GAME. DEER TOE BONES, BASES CUT, HOLLOWED AND DRILLED, WERE STRUNG TO A WOODEN OR BONE NEEDLE SEVERAL INCHES IN LENGTH. WHEN FLIPPED, THE PLAYER TRIED TO CATCH THE BONES IN THE AIR. SINCE THE LOWER BONE COULD REST IN ITS UPPER NEIGHBOR, SEVERAL BONES COULD BE CAUGHT AT THE SAME TIME. THE LOWER THE BONE, THE BETTER THE SCORE.

94

AND for the girls, a preview of motherhood with the help of doll-play. Meanwhile, the boys of the tribe imitated the warriors' games, enthusiasm being substituted for their elders' skill.

TOOLS OF WAR ~

Games were the proving grounds for the aspiring warrior. The increasing frequency of intertribal conflicts called for individual courage and skill. It was every man for himself, for there was usually no over-all strategy. The English observer found these skirmishes far less bloody than European fighting. Cautious stalking, ambushing, dodging arrows and whooping seemed a strange way to do battle. Casualties were modest-perhaps a dozen or so ~ but enough to uphold the honor of the tribe and yet not drastically deplete the relatively small Algonquin population.

The newly arrived colonists were welcomed as allies - a strong arm to be used against a more powerful tribe. Steel knives, iron tomahawks and those wonderous bellowing muskets were formidable answers to bows, arrows and stone weapons. Friendly tribesmen were eager to trade for these modern tools of war, and as early as 1627, the Indians were so well stocked that Governor Bradford worried that guns "...will be the overthrow of all, if it be not looked into." Although the newcomers had little influence over traditional tribal warfare, they certainly made it more efficient.

1 X

1 X

CERAMIC DOLL ~ CAPE COD. BRONSON MUSEUM, ATTLEBORO, MASS.

DEERSKIN DOLL, BELIEVED TO BE NARRAGANSETT. RED-DYED BODY WITH SMALL WHITE BEAD DECORATION. ROGER WILLIAMS MUSEUM, R.I.

ALL 1X

INDIAN MADE IRON AND BRASS ARROWHEADS, FORT SHANTOK. PEABODY MUSEUM, NEW HAVEN, CONNECTICUT.

INDIAN MADE ANTLER HANDLE WITH BRASS BLADED KNIFE.

WINTHROP, MASS. PEABODY MUSEUM, CAMBRIDGE, MASS.

KNIFE OF FRENCH MANUFACTURE FROM THE FIELD OF THE BLOODY BROOK MASSACRE IN 1675. FOUND WHEN A WELL WAS DUG IN 1775. MEMORIAL HALL, OLD DEERFIELD, MASS.

$\frac{3}{4}$ X

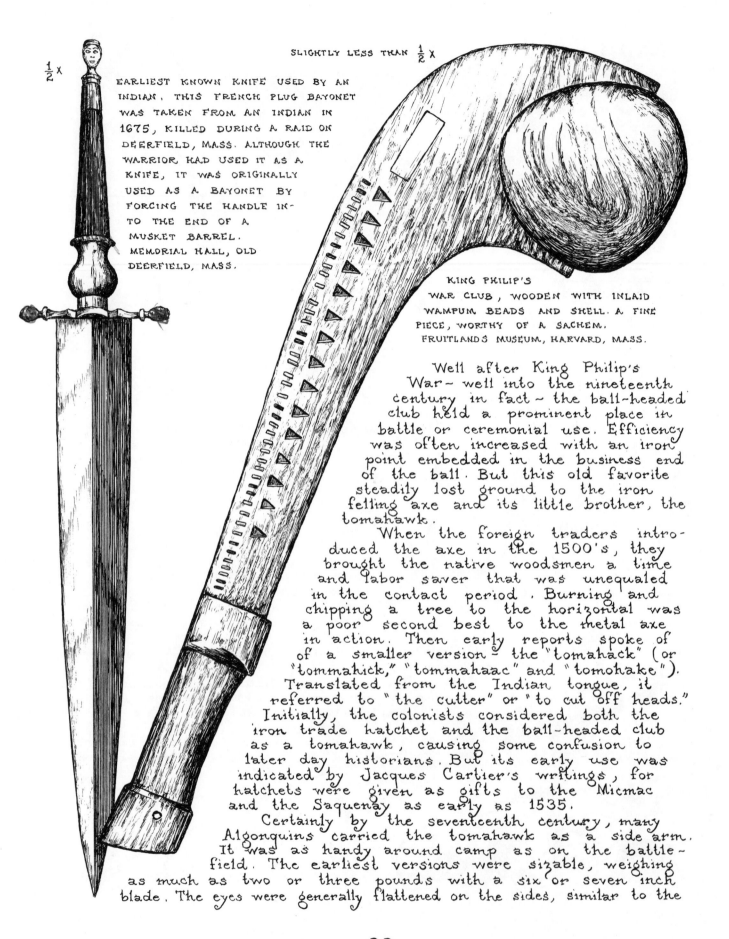

½ X

EARLIEST KNOWN KNIFE USED BY AN
INDIAN, THIS FRENCH PLUG BAYONET
WAS TAKEN FROM AN INDIAN IN
1675, KILLED DURING A RAID ON
DEERFIELD, MASS. ALTHOUGH THE
WARRIOR HAD USED IT AS A
KNIFE, IT WAS ORIGINALLY
USED AS A BAYONET BY
FORCING THE HANDLE IN-
TO THE END OF A
MUSKET BARREL.
MEMORIAL HALL, OLD
DEERFIELD, MASS.

KING PHILIP'S
WAR CLUB, WOODEN WITH INLAID
WAMPUM BEADS AND SHELL. A FINE
PIECE, WORTHY OF A SACHEM.
FRUITLANDS MUSEUM, HARVARD, MASS.

Well after King Philip's
War ~ well into the nineteenth
century in fact ~ the ball-headed
club held a prominent place in
battle or ceremonial use. Efficiency
was often increased with an iron
point embedded in the business end
of the ball. But this old favorite
steadily lost ground to the iron
felling axe and its little brother, the
tomahawk.

When the foreign traders introduced the axe in the 1500's, they
brought the native woodsmen a time
and labor saver that was unequaled
in the contact period. Burning and
chipping a tree to the horizontal was
a poor second best to the metal axe
in action. Then early reports spoke of
of a smaller version ~ the "tomahack" (or
"tommahick," "tommahaac" and "tomohake").
Translated from the Indian tongue, it
referred to "the cutter" or "to cut off heads."
Initially, the colonists considered both the
iron trade hatchet and the ball-headed club
as a tomahawk, causing some confusion to
later day historians. But its early use was
indicated by Jacques Cartier's writings, for
hatchets were given as gifts to the Micmac
and the Saquenay as early as 1535.

Certainly by the seventeenth century, many
Algonquins carried the tomahawk as a side arm.
It was as handy around camp as on the battlefield. The earliest versions were sizable, weighing
as much as two or three pounds with a six or seven inch
blade. The eyes were generally flattened on the sides, similar to the

Saugus specimen. Lighter versions, averaging about five inches from cutting edge to the top of an oval eye, were in common use by King Philip's War.

THE TOMAHAWK WAS SIMPLICITY ITSELF. HOT STRAP IRON WAS HAMMERED AROUND A ROD TO FORM THE EYE.

AFTER WELDING THE EYE CLOSED AND THE ENDS OF THE STRAP FLARED BY POUNDING, A PIECE OF STEEL WAS INSERTED AND JOINED TO THE BODY. GRINDING COMPLETED IT.

17TH CENTURY TOMAHAWKS. $\frac{1}{2}$ X

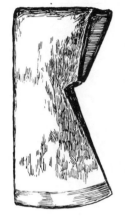

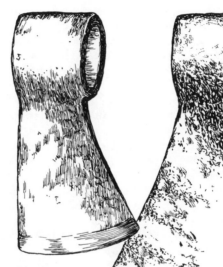
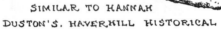
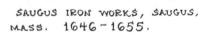

DUTCH - STYLE. FORT SHANTOK, CONN.

FRENCH. CHURCHILL LAKE, MAINE.

ENGLISH - SIMILAR TO HANNAH DUSTON'S. HAVERHILL HISTORICAL SOCIETY, HAVERHILL, MASS. AND SAUGUS IRONWORKS, MASS. 1650±.

SAUGUS IRON WORKS, SAUGUS, MASS. 1646~1655.

ENGLISH. HAFTED AS STONE AXES.

The importance of the tomahawk on the warpath was not diminished by the musket. Once fired, the warrior was helpless until he reloaded his piece. This awkward pause was filled with his side arm. It became a symbol of war, and it was usual to send a tomahawk or a wampum belt with a hand axe design when battle was under consideration or when peace was to be declared.

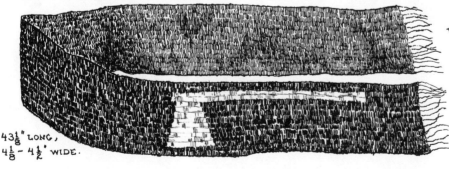

43⅛" LONG, 4⅛ - 4½" WIDE.

BLUE AND WHITE WAMPUM BELT WITH TOMAHAWK DESIGN. THE 15 ROWS OF BEADS WERE STRUNG ON A HEMP WEFT AND A DEERSKIN WARP. PRESENTED TO A DEFEATED ALGONQUIN TRIBE BY THE VICTORIOUS IROQUOIS IN 1670. MUSEUM OF THE AMERICAN INDIAN, HEYE FOUNDATION, NEW YORK CITY.

FORBIDDEN TRADES ~ The most wanted in this bonanza of trade goods was the musket. Here was a power so deadly that it could drop game ~ or perhaps an old enemy tribesman ~ well beyond the reach of an arrow. The Puritan newcomers were well aware of the latter possibility, and that some day the English might be looking down their own musket muzzles. Stiff laws were passed ~ not always successful ~ for a trickle of arms continued from gunrunning fishermen and traders cruising the coast. Occasionally the laws were relaxed for "friendly" natives as in the years just prior to King Philip's War. By 1675, the Algonquins were well supplied with arms and knew how to use them.

The colonists placed spirits in the same forbidden goods category. Peace between the two cultures was very much at stake. Drunken marauding tribesmen could upset fifty years of understanding and cooperation. Although the anti-liquor trade laws were not particularly successful, most native infringements were smoothed by the efficient and impartial Puritan courts.

LAND TRADES ~ Nine thousand years of coping with the wilderness had ceased with the arrival of a more civilized culture. Rugged cutting steel blades ~ efficient farming tools ~ trim clothing ~ warm blankets ~ glass and metal ornaments that no stone or shell work could duplicate ~ they were there for the wanting. Creativity seemed pointless.

The Indians had all the makings for a good trade ~ a plenty of pelts and a land surplus. Outside their planting fields and villages lay vast tracts of unused countryside. Another plague ~ the small pox epidemic of 1633~1634 ~ swept away thousands of Algonquins and made more land available. Only between fifteen to eighteen thousand souls still survived in all of New England. Meanwhile, the patchwork of colonial towns was bulging with new arrivals, eager to start clearing their own piece of America.

Land transfer was not a simple matter. The Puritan laws jealously guarded the rights of the native. Only through qualified agents could purchases be made. Interpreters must be present, as well as several witnesses for both parties. The Indian owner or his family must be present for the formal signing, for unlike the communal tribal lands of the western Indians, much of the land was owned by individual tribesmen. Finally, the sachem must also add his mark if he were in agreement.

If all this puzzled the land-rich warrior, he may have been aware of his rights under English law. And when all was said and done, he generally retained his right to hunt and fish on the property. To the twentieth century mind, trade goods seem a small price to pay for a slice of real estate. But values must be interpreted as to time and place, and the

1 X

POWDER HORN ~
FOUND IN THE
CABIN OF "OLD WARREN",
LAST OF THE PLYMOUTH
INDIANS. PILGRIM MUSEUM,
PLYMOUTH, MASSACHUSETTS.

ENGLISH FLINT MUSKET,
USED BETWEEN 1630-1650.

98

Algonquin was certain he had the best of the bargain.

THE LAST DAYS ~

Not infrequently did whole Indian families desert the remaining tribal lands to begin a new way of life in the Praying Indian towns. They were ready to cast off their old traditions to become Christian Algonquins. But the call to conversion was shunned by the many who held to the old ways. Their chieftains were distressed, for colonial influence had lessened their leadership and power ~ and the tribal tributes considered their due.

Massasoit had long enjoyed a mutual cooperation and protection pact with the neighboring Plymouth Colony. When his son, Philip, became sachem of the Wampanoags, he was determined to restore the independence of his position. He worked mightily for a great uprising that would drive the English into the sea. And it very nearly succeeded. In the fury that tore the years of 1675 and 1676 apart, more than a dozen colonial towns were completely leveled. Many others were barely habitable. A staggering ten percent of the civilians under arms lost their lives in battle.

LOCK OF GUN THAT KILLED PHILIP. MASS. HISTORICAL SOCIETY, BOSTON.

$\frac{2}{5} \pm X$

But in this brief moment in history, the Algonquin people fragmented and dissolved from New England. Five thousand native casualties later, the remnants gave themselves up or fled to old tribal enemies in New York and Canada. Only during the French and Indian Wars did they take the war-path back to their forfeited lands, burning and pillaging the New England frontiers. In the crush of colonial progress and growth that followed, there was little to remind succeeding generations of the centuries of Indian presence.

ENGRAVED BRASS PLAQUE, GIVEN AT A COUNCIL CELEBRATING THE END OF KING PHILIP'S WAR IN 1676. IT WAS PRESENTED BY THE MASSACHUSETTS BAY COLONY TO THE SACHEMS OF THE FRIENDLY TRIBES IN GRATITUDE FOR THEIR ASSISTANCE. IT IS THE ONLY EXAMPLE KNOWN, AND ONE OF THE OLDEST SURVIVING PEACE MEDALS. THE DESIGN LATER BECAME THE OFFICIAL SEAL OF MASSACHUSETTS.

HEYE MUSEUM OF THE AMERICAN INDIAN, N.Y.C.

Yet the early natives left a part of themselves behind ~ from the finely crafted tools to the pendants and beads that brightened their world. Each had its purpose and its own time and place in the Algonquin way of life. If you are fortunate enough to hold a piece of this ancient culture in your hand, let your imagination take hold. Think on its use, efficiency and design ~ and the ingenuity that turned ordinary stone or clay into a tool for survival. You're on your way to knowing these early New Englanders better!

PATTERNS IN STONE ~ OUTLINE IDENTIFICATION.

PA = PALEO AMERICAN. (8500~5000 B.C.)
EA = EARLY ARCHAIC. (5000~3000 B.C.)
LA = LATE ARCHAIC. (3000 B.C ~ 300 A.D.)
C = CERAMIC. (300 A.D. ~ 1676 A.D.)

PROJECTILE POINTS

FLUTED PARALLEL STEM. BIFURCATED LONG EARED CORNER REMOVED

CORNER REMOVED TAPERED STEM TURKEY TAIL EARED —— SIDE NOTCHED ——

DIAMOND —— SMALL TRIANGULAR (BASE LESS THAN 1½ INCHES) —— LARGE TRIANGULAR (BASE MORE THAN 1½) CORNER REMOVED LEAF

ATLATL WEIGHTS ~ SPEAR THROWING WEIGHTS

OVAL WING WHALETAIL BOWTIE

RUBBING STONES ~ GRINDING, GROOVING AND SHARPENING

WHETSTONE ABRADINGSTONE SHAFT ABRADERS SINEWSTONE

SCRAPERS ~ CURVED BLADE, BEVELED ON ONE SIDE

SIDE SCRAPER STEM SHAFT FLAKE OVAL STEEPEDGE

NOTCHERS ~ WORKED LIKE A SAW.   ## POUNDING STONES

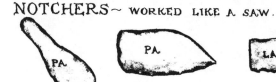  

GRAVERS DENTATE STAMP STYLE PITTED POUNDINGSTONE GROOVED HAMMERSTONE

HAMMERSTONE

MARKING STONES (GRAVERS)

100

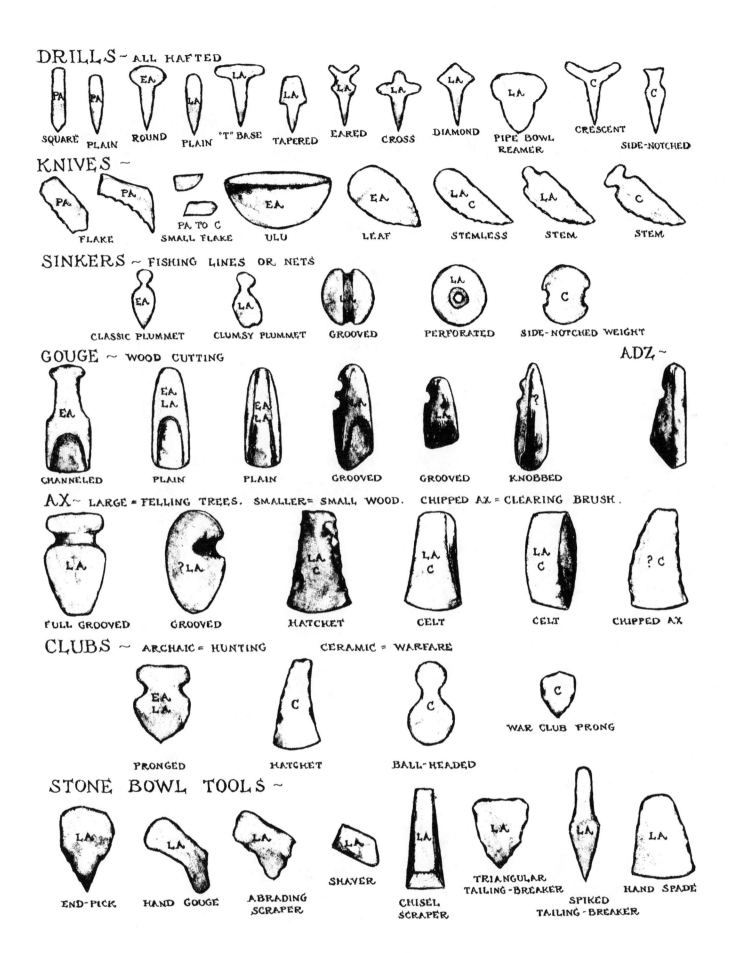

DRILLS ~ ALL HAFTED

SQUARE · PLAIN · ROUND · PLAIN · "T" BASE · TAPERED · EARED · CROSS · DIAMOND · PIPE BOWL REAMER · CRESCENT · SIDE-NOTCHED

KNIVES ~

FLAKE · PA TO C · SMALL FLAKE · ULU · LEAF · STEMLESS · STEM · STEM

SINKERS ~ FISHING LINES OR NETS

CLASSIC PLUMMET · CLUMSY PLUMMET · GROOVED · PERFORATED · SIDE-NOTCHED WEIGHT

GOUGE ~ WOOD CUTTING   ADZ ~

CHANNELED · PLAIN · PLAIN · GROOVED · GROOVED · KNOBBED

AX ~ LARGE = FELLING TREES. SMALLER = SMALL WOOD. CHIPPED AX = CLEARING BRUSH.

FULL GROOVED · GROOVED · HATCHET · CELT · CELT · CHIPPED AX

CLUBS ~ ARCHAIC = HUNTING   CERAMIC = WARFARE

PRONGED · HATCHET · BALL-HEADED · WAR CLUB PRONG

STONE BOWL TOOLS ~

END-PICK · HAND GOUGE · ABRADING SCRAPER · SHAVER · CHISEL SCRAPER · TRIANGULAR TAILING-BREAKER · SPIKED TAILING-BREAKER · HAND SPADE

101

STONE UTENSILS ~ ALL LATE ARCHAIC

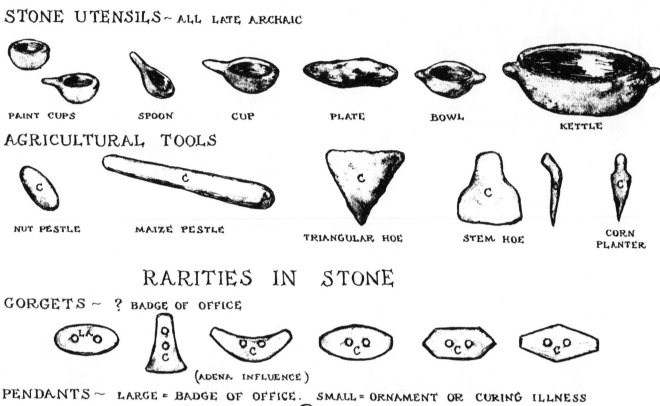

PAINT CUPS   SPOON   CUP   PLATE   BOWL   KETTLE

AGRICULTURAL TOOLS

NUT PESTLE   MAIZE PESTLE   TRIANGULAR HOE   STEM HOE   CORN PLANTER

RARITIES IN STONE

GORGETS ~ ? BADGE OF OFFICE

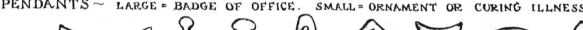

(ADENA INFLUENCE)

PENDANTS ~ LARGE = BADGE OF OFFICE.   SMALL = ORNAMENT OR CURING ILLNESS

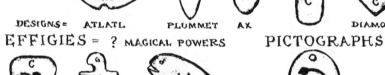

DESIGNS = ATLATL   PLUMMET   AX   DIAMOND   PROJECTILE   OVAL   TRIANGULAR

EFFIGIES = ? MAGICAL POWERS   PICTOGRAPHS   ADENA INFLUENCE

HEAD   HUMAN   FISH   MOVABLE PICTURES   BIRDSTONE   BOATSTONE

FIRE ~ MAKING TOOLS ~

IRON PYRITE   FLINT   HANDLE FOR STICK AND BOW (FRICTION)

PIPES ~ STEATITE

STRAIGHT TUBULAR   STRAIGHT   ELBOW   PLATFORM   BOWL TYPES (HOLE FOR WOODEN STEM)

GAME STONES

STONE BALL   DISCOIDAL   FLATFACED ROLLING   DICE STONE COUNTER

CHOICE OF STONES

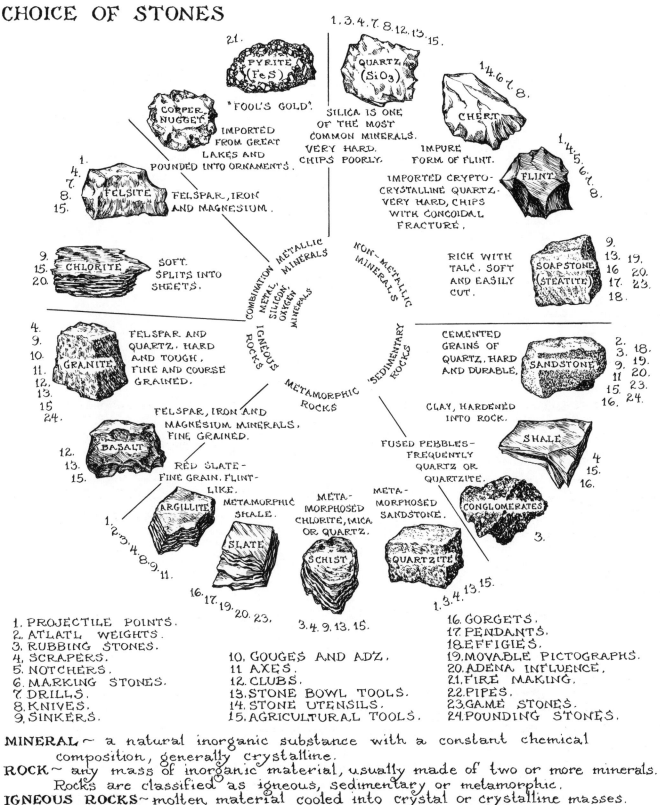

21.

PYRITE (FeS)

"FOOL'S GOLD".

COPPER NUGGET

IMPORTED FROM GREAT LAKES AND POUNDED INTO ORNAMENTS.

1. 3. 4. 7. 8. 12. 13. 15.

QUARTZ (SiO₃)

SILICA IS ONE OF THE MOST COMMON MINERALS. VERY HARD. CHIPS POORLY.

1. 4. 6. 7. 8.

CHERT

IMPURE FORM OF FLINT.

1. 4. 5. 6. 7. 8.

FLINT

IMPORTED CRYPTO-CRYSTALLINE QUARTZ. VERY HARD, CHIPS WITH CONCOIDAL FRACTURE.

1.
4.
7.
8.
15.

FELSITE

FELSPAR, IRON AND MAGNESIUM.

9.
15.
20.

CHLORITE

SOFT. SPLITS INTO SHEETS.

RICH WITH TALC. SOFT AND EASILY CUT.

9.
13. 19.
16. 20.
17. 23.
18.

SOAPSTONE (STEATITE)

COMBINATION METALLIC MINERALS

METAL, SILICON, OXYGEN MINERALS

NON-METALLIC MINERALS

IGNEOUS ROCKS

SEDIMENTARY ROCKS

METAMORPHIC ROCKS

4.
9.
10.
11.
12.
13.
15.
24.

GRANITE

FELSPAR AND QUARTZ. HARD AND TOUGH, FINE AND COURSE GRAINED.

CEMENTED GRAINS OF QUARTZ, HARD AND DURABLE.

2. 18.
3. 19.
9. 20.
11. 23.
15. 24.
16.

SANDSTONE

CLAY, HARDENED INTO ROCK.

FELSPAR, IRON AND MAGNESIUM MINERALS, FINE GRAINED.

12.
13.
15.

BASALT

SHALE

4.
15.
16.

RED SLATE - FINE GRAIN. FLINT-LIKE. METAMORPHIC SHALE.

ARGILLITE

FUSED PEBBLES - FREQUENTLY QUARTZ OR QUARTZITE.

CONGLOMERATES

3.

1. 2. 3. 4. 8. 9. 11.

SLATE

META-MORPHOSED CHLORITE, MICA OR QUARTZ.

META-MORPHOSED SANDSTONE.

16. 17. 19. 20. 23.

SCHIST

QUARTZITE

1. 3. 4. 13. 15.

3. 4. 9. 13. 15.

1. PROJECTILE POINTS.
2. ATLATL WEIGHTS.
3. RUBBING STONES.
4. SCRAPERS.
5. NOTCHERS.
6. MARKING STONES.
7. DRILLS.
8. KNIVES.
9. SINKERS.
10. GOUGES AND ADZ.
11. AXES.
12. CLUBS.
13. STONE BOWL TOOLS.
14. STONE UTENSILS.
15. AGRICULTURAL TOOLS.
16. GORGETS.
17. PENDANTS.
18. EFFIGIES.
19. MOVABLE PICTOGRAPHS.
20. ADENA INFLUENCE.
21. FIRE MAKING.
22. PIPES.
23. GAME STONES.
24. POUNDING STONES.

MINERAL ~ a natural inorganic substance with a constant chemical composition, generally crystalline.

ROCK ~ any mass of inorganic material, usually made of two or more minerals. Rocks are classified as igneous, sedimentary or metamorphic.

IGNEOUS ROCKS ~ molten material cooled into crystal or crystalline masses.

SEDIMENTARY ROCKS ~ layered deposits of sediment such as mud or sand, deposited by gravity, wind, water, and cemented by silica or other minerals.

METAMORPHIC ROCKS ~ igneous or sedimentary rocks, transformed by great heat or pressure.

BIBLIOGRAPHY - THE NEW ENGLAND INDIANS
Note—because of the number, "*MAS*" will refer to
    Massachusetts Archaeological Society Bulletin
    Published by the Massachusetts Archaeological Society,
    Inc.
    Bronson Museum, Attleboro, Mass.

A.

Abbott, John S.
    The History of King Philip
    Harper & Brothers, N.Y. 1857
Adney, Edwin Tappan, and Chapelle, Howard I.
    The Bark Canoes and Skin Boats of North America Museum
    of History and Technology, Smithsonian Institution, Wash-
    ington, D.C. U.S. Government Printing Office, Washing-
    ton: 1964

B.

Barratt, Joseph
    The Indians of New England and the North-Eastern Provinces
    Middletown, Conn. 1851
Berry, George S.
    The Great Shell Mounds of Damariscotta P. 178-88
    New England Magazine Vol. 19, 1898:99
Bodge, George Madison
    Soldiers in King Philip's War 3rd Edition
    Boston, 1906
Borns, Jr., Harold W.
    Possible Paleo-Indian Migration Routes in the North-
    east P. 13-15
    MAS Vol. 34 Nos. 1 and 2 October 1972 - January 1973
Bradford, William
    History of Plymouth Plantation
    Boston 1879

C.

Caverly, Robert B.
    Heroism of Hannah Duston, together with the Indian Wars
    of New England
    B.B. Russell & Co., Boston, 1874
Champlain, Samuel de
    Voyages of Samuel de Champlain 1604-1618
    Edited by W.L. Grant, Original Narratives of Early American
    History
    New York 1907
Chapelle, Howard I.
    The Bark Canoes and Skin Boats of North America Museum
    of History and Technology, Smithsonian Institution, Wash-
    ington, D.C.
    U.S. Government Printing Office, Washington: 1964
Chapin, Howard M.
    Sachems of the Narragansetts P. 66-69 and 75-90
    Rhode Island Historical Society
    Roger Williams Press, E.A. Johnson Co., Providence, 1931
Church, Thomas, Esq.
    History of Philip's War
    With Appendix by Samuel G. Drake
    2nd Edition with Plates
    J.H.A. Frost, Boston, 1827
Connole, Dennis A.
    Land Occupied by the Nipmuck Indians of Central New
    England p. 14-19
    MAS Vol. 38 Nos. 1 and 2 October 1976

D.

DeForest, John W.
    History of the Indians of Connecticut
    Wm. Jas. Hamersley, Hartford, 1851
Dixon, R.B.
    The Early Migrations of the Indians of New England and
    the Maritime Provinces P. 65-76
    Proceedings of the American Antiquarian Society, New Series
    Vol. 24 pt. 1
    Worcester 1914
Dodge, Karl S.
    The Oakholm Site: A Preliminary Report P. 24-27
    MAS Vol. 28 No. 2 Jan. 1967
Drake, Samuel G.
    —Indian Biography
    Published by Josiah Drake at the Antiquarian Bookstore
    56 Cornhill, Boston 1832
    —The Book of the Indians
    Boston, 1824
    —The History of the Indian Wars in New England from the
    First Settlement to the Termination of the War with King
    Philip, in 1677 (2 Vol.)
    Roxbury, Mass. 1865
    —The Old Indian Chronicle . . . and Chronicles of the Indians
    Boston 1836

E.

Eliot, John
    John Eliot's Description of New England in 1650
    Proceedings of the Massachusetts Historical Society 2
    Ser. II
    1885-1886

Ellis, George W., and Morris, John E.
    King Philip's War
    The Grafton Press, New York 1906
Erb, Elmer T.
    Fire: The First Scientific Tool of Man P. 20-23
    MAS Vol. 31 No. 3 and 4 April - July 1970
Everts, Louis H.
    History of The Connecticut Valley in Massachusetts
    Vol I & II
    J.B., Lippincott & Co., Philadelphia 1879

F.

Fenstermaker, G.B.
    Susquehanna, Iroquois Colored Trade Bead Chart
    1575-1763
    Lancaster, Fenstermaker 1974
Field, Edward A.B.
    State of Rhode Island and Providence Plantations at the End
    of the Century:
    A History Vol. I P. 122-129 and 401-421
    The Mason Publishing Company, Boston & Syracuse
    1902
Forbes, Allan
    —Other Indian Events of New England Vol. II
    State Street Trust Company of Boston
    Walton Advertising & Printing Co., Boston, 1941
    —Some Indian Events of New England P. 2-3, 20-25, 74-94
    Printed for the State Street Trust Company of Boston
    Walton Advertising & Printing Co., Boston 1934
Fowler, William S.
    —Adena Culture of Ohio P. 1-4
    MAS Vol. 27 No. 1 October 1965
    —A Case for an Early Archaic in New England P. 53-58
    MAS Vol. 29 Nos. 3 and 4 April - July 1968
    —A Review of Dugout-Making P. 1-6
    MAS Vol. 37 Nos. 1 and 2 October 1975 - January 1976
    —A Study of Projectile Points P. 1-8
    MAS Vol. 35 Nos. 3 and 4 April - July 1974
    —Aboriginal Grinding Equipment P. 19-25
    MAS Vol. 31 Nos. 1 and 2 October 1969 - January 1970
    —Abodes of Four Aboriginal Periods P. 15-22
    MAS Vol. 34 Nos. 3 and 4 April - July 1973
    —Archaic Discoveries at Flat River P. 17-36
    MAS Vol. 29 No. 2 Jan. 1968
    —An Inquiry Into the Contact Stage P. 22-28
    MAS Vol. 37 Nos. 1 and 2 October 1975 - Jan. 1976
    —Bull Brook: A Paleo Complex Site P. 1-6
    MAS Vol. 34 Nos. 1 and 2 October 1972 - January 1973
    —Ceremonial and Domestic Products of Aboriginal New
    England P. 34-68
    MAS Vol. 27 Nos. 3 and 4 April - July 1966
    —Classification of Stone Implements of the Northeast P. 1-29
    MAS Vol. 25 No. 1 October 1963
    —Comparative Study of Hoe and Spade Blades P. 1-9
    MAS Vol. 35 Nos. 1 and 2 October 1973 - January 1974
    —Discoveries at Wilcox Brook Site P. 1-8
    MAS Vol. 36 Nos. 1 and 2 April - July 1967
    —Discovery of Fertilizer in Maize Cultivation P. 23-26
    MAS Vol. 31 Nos. 3 and 4 April - July 1970
    —Division of Labor: Archaeological Disclosures P. 6-12
    MAS Vol. 37 Nos. 1 and 2 October 1975 - January 1976
    —Eating Practices in Aboriginal New England P. 21-27
    MAS Vol. 36 Nos. 3 and 4 April - July 1975
    —Eden Points in Massachusetts P. 29-31
    MAS Vol. 33 Nos. 3 and 4 April - July 1972
    —Figured Art: Its Presence in Stone Age New England P. 20-24
    MAS Vol. 35 Nos. 1 and 2 October 1973 - January 1974
    —Hafting Atlatl Weights P. 15-17
    MAS Vol. 30 No. 2 January 1969
    —Hafting Stone Implements P. 1-12
    MAS Vol. 34 Nos. 3 and 4 April - July 1973
    —Metal Cutouts of the Northeast P. 24-30
    MAS Vol. 34 Nos. 3 and 4 April - July 1973
    —Magic Stones and Shamans P. 10-17
    MAS Vol. 36 Nos. 3 and 4 April - July 1975
    —Maine Archaic Complex P. 10-15
    MAS Vol. 33 Nos. 3 and 4 April - July 1968
    —Mary Rowlandson and Indian Behavior P. 25-31
    MAS Vol. 35 Nos. 3 and 4 April - July 1974
    —New England Tomahawks P. 10-16
    MAS Vol. 31 Nos. 3 and 4 April - July 1970
    —Oaklawn Quarry: Stone Bowl and Pipe Making P. 1-17
    MAS Vol. 29 No. 1 October 1967
    —Procurement and Use of Bark P. 15-19
    MAS Vol. 37 Nos. 1 and 2 October 1975 - January 1976
    —Sharpening Stones P. 28-30
    MAS Vol. 37 Nos. 1 and 2 October 1975 - January 1976
    —Stone Bowl-Making at the Westfield Quarry P. 6-16
    MAS Vol. 30 No. 1 October 1968
    —Some Sources of New England Flints P. 23-28
    MAS Vol. 32 Nos. 3 and 4 April - July 1971
    —Ten Thousand Years in America
    Vantage Press, New York 1957
    —The Diagnostic Stone Bowl Industry P. 1-9
    MAS Vol. 36 Nos. 3 and 4 April - July 1975
    —The Making of Wing Atlatl Weights P. 19-21
    MAS Vol. 36 Nos. 1 and 2 October 1974 - January 1975
    —The Wilbraham Stone Bowl Quarry P. 9-22
    MAS Vol. 30 Nos. 3 and 4 April - July 1969

G.

Gookin, Daniel
    —An Historical Account of the Doings and Sufferings of the
    Christian Indians of New England P. 423-534
    Transactions and Collections of the American Antiquarian
    Society
    Cambridge, Mass. 1836
    —The Historical Collections of the Indians in New England
    (Reprinted from Massachusetts Historical Society Collections.
    Originally written by Gookin in 1674)
    Spencer, Mass. 1970
Goulding, Stuart D.
    Deep in the Rhode Island Forest P. 42-48
    Yankee Magazine March 1969
    Published by Yankee, Inc., Dublin, N.H. 1969
Griffin, James B.
    "Eastern North America, The Northeast Woodlands Area,"
    Prehistoric Man in the New World. Jennings, Jesse D., and
    Edward Norbeck, editors. P. 223-225. The University of
    Chicago Press, Chicago & London. Published 1964. Fifth
    Impression 1971
Gringhuis, Dirk
    Indian Costume at Mackinac: Seventeenth And Eighteenth
    Century
    Mackinac History Vol. II Leaflet No. 1
    Published by Mackinac Island State Park Commission
    Mackinac Island, Michigan 1972

H.

Hadlock, Wendell S., and Butler Eva L.
    Uses of Birch Bark in the Northeast
    Robert Abbe Museum, Bulletin No. 7
    Bar Harbor, Maine 1957
Haviland, William A.
    Gorgets: Ornamental or Utilitarian? P. 30-32
    MAS Vol. 31 Nos. 3 and 4 April - July 1970
Holmes, William H.
    Handbook of Aboriginal American Antiquities Part I
    Bull. 60
    Bureau of American Ethnology
    Washington, D.C. 1919
Howe, Henry F.
    Early Explorers of Plymouth Harbor 1525-1619
    Published jointly by Plimoth Plantation, Inc. and the Pilgrim
    Society, Plymouth 1953
    The Meriden Gravure Company, Meriden, Connecticut
Hubbard, William
    —A General History of New England
    Massachusetts Historical Society Collections 2 Ser. V-VI
    Boston 1815
    —A Narrative of the Troubles with the Indians in New-England
    Boston, 1677 (Also edition pub. Brattleborough 1814)
Huden, John C., compiled by
    Archaeology in Vermont, Revised Edition
    Charles E. Tuttle Co., Rutland, Vt. 1971
    Printed in Japan
Hume, Ivor Noel
    A Guide to Artifacts of Colonial America P. 53-54
    Alfred A. Knopf, New York 1970
Hutchinson, Mr. (Thomas) Lieutenant-Governor of the Massa-
    chusett's Province
    The History of the Colony of Massachusetts Bay, The Second
    Edition
    Printed for M. Richardson in Pater-Noster Row,
    London 1765

J.

Jack, Edward
    "Malecite Legends" P. 200
    Journal of American Folklore Vol. VIII No. 20 1895
Josephy, Alvin M.
    The Patriot Chiefs
    Viking Press, N.Y. 1961
Josselyn, John
    An Account of Two Voyages to New-England, London 1675
    P. 211-354
    Republished in the Collections of the Massachusetts Historical
    Society, Third Series Vol. III
    Cambridge, 1833

K.

Karklins, Karlis, and Roderick Sprague
    Glass Trade Beads in North America: An Annotated Biblio-
    graphy P. 87-101
    Historical Archaeology Vol. 6 1972
Kevitt, Chester B.
    Aboriginal Dugout Recovered at Weymouth P. 1-5
    MAS Vol. 30 No. 1 October 1968

M.

MacGowan, Kenneth, and Joseph, Hester A., Jr.
    Early Man in the New World
    The Natural History Library, Anchor Books
    Doubleday & Co., Inc. Garden City, N.Y.
    The Natural History Library Edition 1962

Mason, Otis T.
—Indian Basketry Vol. II P. 272, 276-277
Doubleday, Page and Co., 1904
—Origin of Invention
Charles Scribner's Sons, New York 1895
—Traps of the American Indians - A Study in Psychology and
Invention P. 461-474
Annual Report of the Board of Regents of the Smithsonian
Institution. The Year Ending June 30, 1901
Washington Government Printing Office 1902
Mather, Increase
A Brief History of the War with the Indians in New-England,
Boston & London 1676
Edited by Samuel Drake under the title The History of King
Philip's War.
Boston, 1862
Mayhew, Experience
Observations on the Indian Language
Published from the Manuscript by John S.H. Fogg, Boston 1884
McGimsey, Charles R. III
Stone Working: Fracturing or Chipping P. 60-64
Courtesy of Arkansas Archaeological Society News Letter,
Vol. 2, No. 7, Sept. 1961
MAS Vol. 24, Nos. 3 and 4 April - July 1963
Miller, William J.
King Philip and the Wampanoags of Rhode Island
Second Edition
Sidney S. Rider, Providence, 1885
Moffett, Ross
An Unusual Indian Harpoon from Truro P. 22-24
MAS Vol. 30 Nos. 3 and 4 April - July 1969
Moorehead, Warren K.
—A Report on the Archaeology of Maine
Andover, Mass. 1922
—Stone Ornaments
The Andover Press, Andover, Mass. 1922
—The Stone Age in North America 2 Vol.
Cambridge 1910
Morton, Thomas
The New English Canaan
Edited by Charles Francis Adams, Jr.
Publications of the Prince Society XIV Boston 1883

O.

Otis, Leo Derwood
The Proto-Historic Indians of Springfield and Vicinity
Bulletin No. 7
Museum of Natural History, Springfield, Mass. 1950

P.

Painter, Floyd
The Cattail Creek Fluting Tradition P. 6-12
MAS Vol. 34 Nos. 1 and 2 October 1972 - January 1973
Pease, John C., and Niles, John M.
A Gazetteer of the States of Connecticut and Rhode Island
P. 305-389
Published by William S. Marsh, Hartford 1819
Peirce, Ebenezer W.
Indian History, Biography and Geneology
Published by Zervish Gould Mitchell, North Arlington,
Mass. 1878
Peterson, Harold L.
—American Indian Tomahawks
Museum of The American Indian, Heye Foundation 1965
Printed in Germany at J.J. Augustin, Glückstadt.
—American Knives
Charles Scribner's Sons, New York 1958
—Arms and Armor in Colonial America 1526-1783
The Stackpole Co., Harrisburg, Pa. 1956
Potter Jr., Elisha R.
The Early History of Narragansett P. 78-100
Collections of the Rhode-Island Historical Society Vol. III
Providence: Marshall, Brown and Company 1835
Pratt, Peter P.
Oneida Iroquois Glass Trade Bead Sequence 1585-1745
Indian Glass Trade Beads Color Guide Series No. 1
Printed by Onondaga Printing Company, Syracuse New
York 1961

R.

Ray, Roger B.
—Maine Indians Concept of Land Tenure P. 28-51
Maine Historical Society Quarterly Vol. 13 No. 1
Summer 1973
Published at 485 Congress Street, Portland, Maine

—The Indians of Maine: A Bibliographical Guide
The Maine Historical Society
Portland, Maine 1972
Ritchie, William A.
—Indian History of New York State
Part III - The Algonkian Tribes
Educational Leaflet No. 8
New York Museum and Science Service, Albany, N.Y.
(no date)
—The Archaeology of New York State
Published for the American Museum of Natural History
The Natural History Press, Garden City, New York 1965
Rivard, Jean-Jacques, editor and Fowler, William S., illustrator
A Handbook of Indian Artifacts from Southern New England
Massachusetts Archaeological Society, Inc. 1976
Robbins, Maurice
—A Brass Kettle Recovery at Corn Hill, Cape Cod P. 62-68
MAS Vol. 29 Nos. 3 and 4 April - July 1968
—Some Early House Floors P. 1-12
MAS Vol. 32 Nos. 1 and 2 October 1970 - January 1971
—The Titicut Site P. 33-76
MAS Vol. 28 Nos. 3 and 4 April - July 1967
Robinson, Donald, photographs by
Arrowhead flaking techniques at Plimoth Plantation
Plimoth Plantation 1963
Rowlandson, Mrs. Mary
Narrative of the Captivity of Mrs. Mary Rowlandson,
Charles H. Lincoln, ed. Narratives of the Indian Wars
New York 1913
Rush, Benjamin
An Inquiry into the Natural History of Medicine
Among the Indians of North America: And a Comparative
View of their Diseases and Remedies With Those of Civilized
Nations.
Medical Inquiries and Observations Vol. I P. 103-107
N. D.
Russell, Howard S.
New England Agriculture from Champlain and Others
P. 11-18
MAS Vol. 31 Nos. 1 and 2 October 1969 - January 1970

S.

Schneider, Richard C.
Crafts of the North American Indians
A Craftsman's Manual
Van Nostrand Reinhold Company, New York, Cincinnati,
Toronto, London, Melbourne 1972
Schoolcraft, H.R.
History of the Indian Tribes of the United States Vol. 6
Section: 6 Synopsis of the History of the New England Tribes
Philadelphia 1857
Scothorne, Donald G.
A Cache of Bone Implements P. 28-30
MAS Vol. 31 Nos. 1 and 2 October 1969 - January 1970
Sears, Clara Endicott
The Great Powwow
Houghton-Mifflin Co., Boston and New York 1934
Sheldon, George
The Flintlock Used in Philip's War P. 3-28
Reprint from the Proceedings of the Worcester Society of
Antiquity 1900
Shulsinger, Stephanie Cooper
What's In A Place Name? P. 50-53
Yankee Magazine June 1972
Yankee, Inc. Dublin, N.H.
Simmons, Dr. William S., III
The Ancient Graves of Conanicut Island P. 153-175
Newport History
Bulletin of the Newport Historical Society No. 128
Autumn 1967 Vol. 40, Part 4
Printed by Wilkinson Press, Inc. Newport, Rhode Island
Smith, Nicholas N.
—Indian Medicine: Fact or Fiction?
MAS Vol. 26. No. 1 October 1964
—Observations on Eastern Algonkian Linguistics P. 4-8
MAS Vol. 28 No. 1 October 1966
Snow, Dean R.
A Summary of Excavations at the Hathaway Site in
Passadumkeag, Maine. 1912, 1947, 1968
University of Maine, Department of Anthropology,
Orono 1969
Spiess, Mathias
Connecticut Circa 1625. Its Indian Trails Villages and
Sachemdoms
Published by the National Society of the Colonial Dames of
America in the State of Connecticut 1934
Starbird, Charles M.
The Indians of the Androscoggin Valley
Lewiston 1928

Stuart, George E., and Stuart, Gene S.
Discovering Man's Past in the Americas
Published by the National Geographic Society,
Washington, D.C. 1969

T.

Taylor, William B.
A Bifurcated Point Concentration 36-41
MAS Vol. 37 Nos. 3 and 4 April - July 1976
Thomas, Lieutenant Nathaniel
Acct of ye Fight with ye Indians Augt 1t 1675 by Nath l.
dated 10 Aug 1675
Original Letter Massachusetts Historical Society
Davis Papers Mss. 161, G 28

V.

Van Dusen, Albert E.
Connecticut
Random House, N.Y. 1961
Vaughan, Alden T.
New England Frontier: Puritans and Indians 1620-1675
Little Brown and Co., Boston and Toronto 1965
Verarzanus, John
The Relation of Hakluyt's Divers Voyage 1582
Hakluyt reprint
Verrill, A. Hyatt
The American Indian
The New Home Library
D. Appleton and Co., N.Y. 1927

W.

Weeks, Alvin G.
Massasoit
Plimpton Press, Norwood, Mass 1919 (private printing)
Williams, H.V.
The Epidemic of the Indians of New England
1616-1620 with Remarks on Native American Infections
p. 340-349
Johns Hopkins Hospital Bulletin: 20 1909
Williams, Roger
A Key into the Language of America
Fifth Edition
London: Printed by Gregory Dexter, 1643
Reprinted at Providence for The Rhode Island and Providence
Plantations Tercentenary Committee, Inc. 1936
The Roger Williams Press, E.A. Johnson Co., Providence, R.I.
Williamson, William D.
Indian Tribes in New England P. 92-100
Massachusetts Historical Society Collections, Series 3
Vol. 9
Boston, 1846
Willoughby, Charles C.
—Antiquities of the New England Indians
Published by the Peabody Museum of American
Archaeology and Ethnology
Harvard University 1935
—Dress and Ornaments of the New England Indians
P. 499-508
American Anthropologist N.S. 7, 1905
—Prehistoric Burial Places in Maine
Peabody Museum of Harvard University
Archaeological and Ethnological Papers, Vol. 1, No. 6
July 1898
Wilson, Charles B.
Indian Relics and Encampments in Maine P. 181-183
American Antiquarian and Oriental Journal Vol. 5 1883
Winthrop, John
History of New England 1630-1649 2 Vol.
Edited by James K. Hosmer
Original Narratives of Early American History. New York 1908
Wissler, Clark
Indian Costumes in the United States
Guide Leaflet Series No. 63
The American Museum of Natural History, N.Y. July 1926
Wood, William
Wood's New-England's Prospect
Publications of the Prince Society, I. Boston 1865

Y.

Young, William R., Editor
An Introduction to The Archeology and History of the
Connecticut Valley Indian
New Series Vol. 1 No. 1
A Publication of the Springfield Museum of Science 1969

Index